T0311557

Becoming a Kink Aware Therapist

As a result of recent media interest, the practice of BDSM has become more mainstream yet remains marginalized. Now more than ever, greater numbers of heterosexual and LGBTQ couples are starting to explore some form of BDSM. However, profound misunderstandings continue, leading to unintentional physical and psychological harm.

Drawing on current research and ethnographic narratives from the kink community, this book seeks to provide psychotherapists with an introductory understanding of the culture and practice of BDSM, and presents specific therapeutic concerns related to common misconceptions. This book strives to de-pathologize BDSM practices, while also providing concrete ways to distinguish abuse from consent, harmful codependency, and more. Packed with practical suggestions and rich case studies, this book belongs on the shelf of every therapist seeing BDSM and kink clients.

Caroline Shahbaz, BBSc (Hons), MPsych, MA, is a trained clinical psychologist. She has spoken widely at conferences across the US and Australia on issues related to BDSM relationships, consensual master slave dynamics, and kinkophobia as it applies to the practice of psychotherapy.

Peter Chirinos, MA, LPC, NCC, DCC, is the president and CEO of Capital Counseling Services, LLC, where he provides psychotherapy services as well as professional coaching, training, and expert consultations in the area of sex, intimacy, and alternative sexualities.

Becoming a Kink Aware Therapist

Caroline Shahbaz and Peter Chirinos

Routledge
Taylor & Francis Group
New York London

First published 2017
by Routledge
605 Third Avenue, New York, NY 10017

and by Routledge
2 Park Square, Milton Park, Abingdon, Oxon, OX14 4RN

First issued in paperback 2021

Routledge is an imprint of the Taylor & Francis Group, an informa business

© 2017 Taylor & Francis

Publisher's Note
The publisher has gone to great lengths to ensure the quality of this reprint but points out that some imperfections in the original copies may be apparent.

Library of Congress Cataloging in Publication Data

A catalog record for this title has been requested

ISBN 13: 978-1-03-209755-8 (pbk)
ISBN 13: 978-1-138-23965-4 (hbk)

Typeset in Times New Roman PS

by diacriTech

This book is dedicated to all those who have been othered and all therapists who have the courage to explore and face their own fears in order to accept the other in their clients.

Contents

Figures

Tables

Foreword

Margie Nichols, Ph.D.

There is no doubt that in the twenty-first century we are undergoing a sea change in how both the culture at large and the mental health community view sex and gender diversity. Particularly striking is the dramatic upsurge of interest in what used to be called the paraphilias and now are more commonly labeled BDSM, kink, leather, or fetishism.

Much of this interest was sparked by the publication and subsequent runaway success of E. L. James's novel describing a romantic and erotic BDSM relationship, *Fifty Shades of Grey*, in 2011. The book has sold, at last count, upwards of 125 million copies, the movie has to date earned nearly $600 million in box office receipts, and both have triggered a 400 percent increase in the sales of sex toys. E. L. James's own brand of sex toys are sold in Target.

In the wake of this success, researchers are discovering that kinky desires and behaviors are more common than we thought. Research published in the July 2016 issue of the *Journal of Sex Research* indicates that nearly half of Canadian adults surveyed expressed interest in at least one paraphilic category, as taken from the DSM 5, and approximately one-third had experienced a kinky practice at least once.[1] Other research is showing a prevalence of kinky sexual fantasies of as high as 64 percent of adults, depending on the gender and the fantasy.

In the psychiatric world, the publication of DSM 5 in 2013 represented a radical departure from the past. For the first time, having paraphilic interests was not pathologized – being kinky does not equate to being mentally ill. These changes parallel the removal of the diagnosis of homosexuality from the DSM in 1973. In 1973, the combination of the change in psychiatric nomenclature and the increased social acceptance led to more gay people coming out, more exploring hidden desires – and more seeking therapy that affirmed rather than condemned them. Similarly, right now we are seeing an uptick in the number of long-term practitioners of BDSM who are 'coming out,' an increase in the number of those who are translating secret fantasies into experimentation. This is also resulting in larger numbers of kinky people seeking treatment from therapists who will not pathologize their sexuality.

In the 1970s, these events culminated in the development of gay affirmative psychotherapy. Gay affirmative therapy started from the assumption that homosexuality was a normal variation of human behavior, not a mental illness, and then went on to tackle issues specific to lesbian and gay people like homophobia, identity development, and relationships.

We are now at the same point in the development of a new, kink-aware, kink-affirmative, and kink-knowledgeable psychotherapy. And we have a tremendous need for texts to help us in that task. The majority of therapists practicing today were trained in the pathology model of paraphilias and are light years away from really understanding this common – but, until recently, hidden – sexual variation.

Into that vacuum has entered Caroline Shahbaz and Peter Chirinos's book, *Becoming a Kink Aware Therapist*. The book lives up to its title. It is the first capable of taking an interested but wholly unexposed and untrained therapist through a process that will result in the ability to handle some complex therapeutic issues – or to know when those issues need referral to someone more experienced. Shahbaz and Chirinos have a commanding understanding of the research and clinical literature. They use their resources to persuade, through rational argument, those therapists who may not understand the paradigm shift within their own profession. The authors quickly and effectively demolish the pathology model by marshalling the scientific evidence used to change DSM-5. They counter myths and common preconceptions about kink with solid facts and explain the latest research on the psychobiology of BDSM; they sketch a picture with data of typical practitioners and vividly describe the social persecution and discrimination faced by kinksters. The book is worth reading for the psychoeducational information alone, including the appendices and resources at the end.

But Shahbaz and Chirinos go much further than information. They deconstruct kinkophobia and guide the reader in exploring personal biases, and then dig deeper into the common issues encountered in therapy. They cover difficult situations like discerning consent, differentiating between domestic violence and kink, and determining whether a client's behavior constitutes destructive self-injury or merely intense sensation play.

Most impressively, the authors discuss the use of BDSM as a method for healing past traumas, for deepening insight and self-understanding, and for peak experiences and spiritual transformation. These are little explored areas. Here, Shahbaz and Chirinos describe how kink is not merely 'normal' but also contains elements that can foster positive growth in individuals and couples who practice BDSM.

Becoming a Kink Aware Therapist is clear and readable, and contains concrete, pragmatic suggestions for interventions, including a helpful and extremely comprehensive checklist for diagnosing healthy BDSM behavior. The case presentations are engaging, vivid, and relevant.

I do a lot of trainings for sex therapists on sex and gender diversity, including kink and other variations that make up the 'Q' in LGBTQ. In the future, I will be including this book as a primary text for any therapist wishing to learn enough to work with the emerging population of people engaging in BDSM practices.

Margie Nichols, Ph.D.
Founder/President
Institute for Personal Growth
Psychologist and sex therapist, trainer, writer on sex
and gender diversity issues, including BDSM/kink
www.ipgcounseling.com
mnichols@ipgcounseling.com

Note

1   Joyal, C. & Carpenter, J. (2016). The prevalence of paraphilic interests and behaviors in the general population: a provincial survey. *Journal of Sex Research*, July, 3, 1–11.

Foreword

Barry McCarthy, Ph.D.

Becoming a Kink Aware Therapist is a much-needed book on an understudied and misunderstood clinical issue. Traditionally, sex therapy had focused on married and partnered couples who experience problems of desire, arousal, or orgasm. The study of atypical or variant sexual desire and arousal has featured a psychopathology bias and treatment of the "identified patient." In contrast, Shahbaz and Chirinos have written an insightful book for therapists with a focus on a respectful understanding of the culture and practice of BDSM.

The practice of psychotherapy, as all health professions, starts with the dictum "first, do no harm." Sadly, this is not the reality of traditional approaches to BDSM. This has led to unintentional emotional harm to individuals and couples. The lack of scientific data and understanding has led to assumptions of pathology about BDSM which are not supported by research or clinical data.

Becoming a Kink Aware Therapist presents current psychological, relational, and cultural research on the topic of BDSM with an emphasis on de-pathologizing BDSM practices. Individual clients and couples who practice BDSM deserve first-class mental health and sexual health services. Rather than pretending that all clinicians can provide competent treatment for all clients, the new understanding is that the couple/client deserve access to a clinician who is interested in BDSM issues, is well trained and competent in dealing with BDSM problems, and perhaps most importantly, the clinician's personal and professional values are congruent with the clients' goals and values. When this is not true, the clinician makes a referral to a therapist who is interested, competent, and whose values are congruent with BDSM so the clients are in good hands.

A crucial factor is that the therapist conduct a comprehensive assessment rather than assume psychopathology. The Shahbaz-Chirinos checklist for diagnosing healthy BDSM behavior is particularly valuable for clinicians. The clinical assessment and diagnosis need to be based on objective psychological and psychiatric analysis rather than on personal bias or cultural stereotypes. Clinicians need psychological, relational, and sexual competence in dealing with BDSM issues.

A particularly important issue in this book is the exploration of personal and professional discomfort in dealing with BDSM issues. The client/couple deserve to be treated as first-class people so that they can develop healthy patterns which ensure that sexuality has a positive 15 to 20 percent role in their life and relationship. This includes the ability to confront clients where abuse or manipulation is subverting consensual BDSM. Communication, consent, and boundaries are the bedrock of healthy BDSM.

In addition to BDSM, other kink-friendly therapeutic approaches to nontraditional sexuality will benefit from this book. This includes fetishes, cross-dressing, use of erotic scenarios and techniques, acceptance of gender and sexual orientation fluidity, as well as consensual non-monogamy (open relationships, open or closed swinging, and polyamory). A strength of the sexuality field is the recognition of individual differences. An adage is that "in sexuality, one size never fits all."

The Shahbaz and Chirinos book is the premier clinical book which honors healthy, nontraditional sexuality, especially BDSM.

Barry McCarthy, Ph.D.
Professor of Psychology, American University
Author of Sex Made Simple *and* Rekindling Desire

Preface

Caroline's inspiration for this book has its genesis in four disparate foci: the experience of being othered, marginalized sexualities, spirituality, and socially responsible psychology.

As a third-generation survivor of the Armenian genocide, Caroline developed an enduring interest in understanding how marginalization, demonization, and persecution lends itself to the formation of identity and community. While many instances of genocide and hate persist today, the social discrimination and persecution of people with atypical sexualities increasingly came into focus as having a parallel journey, noticing shared qualities and characteristics among *all* who are marginalized and persecuted for being who they are, the 'other.' The categorizing of the other, the systemizing of othering consciousness, in particular through the use of psychological frameworks, to pathologize this new other came into jarring focus for her. These embodied insights are reflected in this book.

In 1987, following a crisis of faith in cognitive behavioral psychology, she experienced a calling to explore the 'road less travelled,' the intersection between spirituality and psychology. Hungry to understand these dimensions of 'psyche' cognitive psychology had abandoned prompted in her an almost obsessive journey to explore what motivates and drives hidden desires and passions and how unresolvable betrayals, pains, and traumas, most notably experienced through othering, can be resolved. That journey led Caroline to Indian gurus, Pilipino faith healers, Buddhist temples, Peruvian shamans, Sufi teachers, and Jung. Ultimately, she came to embrace depth psychology as a different lens with which to see into that which was hidden beneath the surface of consciousness, and a tool to query into marginalized places. Depth psychology provided a framework to explore the edges of socially and culturally accepted places – the places people who are marginalized and othered inhabit like shadows.

In 2003 she was fortunate to meet an exceptional group of people who had dedicated themselves to building a Master slave community; a subgroup of a subgroup of a sexually marginalized community. What was most striking to her was their curiosity, their intense intelligence, their fierce desire for authenticity and too, how similar this phenomenon was to the journey of those who identified as gay thirty years earlier. The importance of authentic community as nurturance and central to identity became clearer. In exploring the BDSM world and the lived experiences of the people in it, Caroline was privileged to witness extraordinary acts of personal courage, authenticity, and intelligent edge living. The lived spaces of those who are sexually marginalized teems with vitality. She witnessed a constant amoeba-like movement in innovative social and relational ideas, interests, and shared experiences in the formation and dissolution of groups seeking community. She understood the embodied, conscious exploration of the edges of pain and pleasure has no equivalent social or cultural phenomenon outside of these marginalized communities. This world was, until now, hidden from mainstream psychology.

A firewall exists between these sexually marginalized groups, erected on their part for self-protection from the misunderstanding and, often, unconscious projections from the professional psychotherapeutic communities. Two experiences define Caroline's desire to breach this wall.

The first was in 2008 at the start of a doctoral journal, a series of clear-headed and openhearted questions one of her cohorts posed to better understand the experience of the lived realities of the BDSM world. These questions were central to the nature of openhearted inquiry and guided her attempt to bridge the therapeutic divide. The second occurrence demonstrated the opposite and was encapsulated in a negative reaction of a group of Jungian psychologists to the spanking scene in the 2011 film *A Dangerous Method*. This served as a lightning rod for the urgency to bring awareness about institutionalized kinkophobia into psychotherapy. The call to create a bridge between sexually marginalized communities and psychotherapeutic communities and to debunk decades of malpractice grew louder and louder. She believes psychology and, in particular, psychotherapy has a duty to lean into, listen, understand, and enhance authentic expression of psyche for individuals and groups. Too, it has a social responsibility to support, not pathologize and therefore reinforce, the process of othering that which it finds difficult to comprehend. It is a positive sign that there is a small but growing number of professionals seeking to understand this marginalized sexual phenomenon.

Working with a broad range of clients with complex clinical issues led Peter to the realization that psychotherapeutic models need new ways of treating disorders to facilitate true profound healing. Several incidents resulted in him becoming disillusioned by a number of facets in the practice of psychotherapy.

Recently, he witnessed a female presenter at a professional training teach the audience to diagnose female partners of philandering men with PTSD, absent of any actual life-threatening event. At that point, the extent of unquestioned ideology imbedded in the practice of psychotherapy became clear to him. This incident demonstrates not just unconscious misandry within the profession, but highlights a pattern within the psychotherapeutic field, in which there is a tendency to other male sexuality, as well as atypical sexualities which, on the surface, do not appear to conform to an ideologically or culturally appropriate expression of intimacy. Similarly, he found numerous theoretical approaches in therapy resulting in minimal meaningful long-term effects. Sadly, oftentimes the predominate focus in psychotherapy is centered on mitigating the potential of therapist liability for treating high-risk and/or complex clients.

Through his clinical practice, he came to recognize that regardless of what clients' presenting concerns were, there was usually an underlying and common core issue: a feeling of not being *seen* and not feeling accepted for who they are by those closest to them. He continuously saw clients desperately living double lives, for example, while living with shame, guilt, and depression. His practice increasingly shifted to facilitate clients' movement to courageously living more authentically with themselves and those around them.

Through these and other experiences, it became clear to him the practice of traditional/mainstream psychotherapy is limited with respect to transpersonal issues and the use of community as a vehicle for transformation. He believes concerns regarding litigation, commercial drives, and the medicalization of the counseling profession have systematically and vehemently discouraged clinicians' willingness to explore alternative nontraditional therapeutic interventions and resulted in a diminished focus on social responsibility and engagement with community. As a result, he is an advocate for alternative models of not just treatment but also personal transformation involving acceptance as well as complementary and alternative practices. When presenting professional workshops on atypical sexualities, Peter has been encouraged by the growing interest in what was, until recently, a baffling denial to understand.

Simultaneously, Peter's exploration into alternative sexualities and empathy for the other comes from a personal dimension. As a bisexual son of a Peruvian father and a German mother, his life experiences embody the *other*. As a first-generation American, he has traversed numerous communities and cultures, sometimes concurrently or in opposition with each other, but never truly being one of the community. It is with this knowledge, understanding, humility, and acceptance he writes this book.

Both Caroline and Peter have ironically observed over the years that while these two disparate bodies, psychotherapy and BDSM, occupy different worlds, they inhabit common meeting places: the conference rooms and halls in hotels across the world where they gather, in which, like ships in the dark, they blithely sail past each other. This book brings the varied BDSM communities and the world occupied by psychotherapists and other professionals together. It offers an invitation to bridge the abyss between these two disparate worlds.

Acknowledgments

We wish to express our gratitude to all those in the BDSM community who have the courage to boldly live and express their unique authenticity and share themselves with us. Their stories and lives enrich ours, and will hopefully expand the professional understanding of this atypical sexuality within the field of psychotherapy. We especially want to thank Susan Wright of the National Coalition of Sexual Freedom (NCSF) and Raven Kaldera for their editorial input, guidance, and encouragement.

Introduction

Since 2010, there has been a maelstrom of media buzz about alternative sexualities such as bondage, discipline, and sadomasochism (BDSM). There is a bewildering number of contradictory information, most often from unreliable sources, which lead to profound confusion and controversy within professional communities. These heated and highly controversial perspectives leave psychotherapists and others in clinical practice with more questions than answers pertaining to emerging definitions of 'normal' and healthy identity structures verses ones that are pathological in nature. Other professional challenges are further complicated when counselors' personal discomfort is fueled by fear due to ignorance and misinformation. This misinformation and fear infiltrate sound professional practice as bias that further feeds controversy.

The information presented in *Becoming a Kink Aware Therapist* will provide an initial introduction into understanding the most essential concepts related to emerging definitions of healthy sexuality, specifically BDSM, in clinical settings. While it focuses on BDSM, many of the principles outlined relate to numerous atypical sexualities: polyamory, bisexuality, mixed orientation relationships, transgender, and gender nonconformity. Most essentially, the book's strength enables the reader to skillfully work with the 'other.'

Book chapters have been created and structured around the essential and most commonly asked 'hot-button' questions from psychotherapists attending various workshops the authors have presented globally. Chapter 1 introduces how healthy sexuality is currently defined and offers a newly reimagined definition.

Psychotherapists also frequently ask for basic information: "What is BDSM?" "What do they do and how is consent given?" Attendees are curious, confused, yet starving to learn about the variety of subcultures, language, and definitions that define this misunderstood sexual minority. Chapter 2 outlines the scope and nature of BDSM, how it is defined and practiced. Special attention to the role of ritual, symbolism, and language within various subcultures are emphasized in order to underscore the subtlety and complexity inherent in understanding the cultural phenomenon of BDSM. In Chapter 2 the intersection between altered states of consciousness experienced by many BDSM practitioners is introduced.

Naturally, many psychotherapists seek clarity about the various paraphilic disorders defined within the DSM-5 and how these affect practice. In Chapter 3 the authors explore the empirical evidence for the paraphilias and the psychopathology within the practice of BDSM. The increasing amount of research calling into question the historic pathologizing of BDSM alongside demographic data pertaining to social discrimination and persecution of people who practice BDSM from legal, medical, and psychological communities is also presented. In Chapter 4 Shahbaz and Chirinos provide readers guidelines that facilitate reflection on counselors' practice when confronted with personally shocking or jarring information from their clients. By developing the ability to discern how and when personal attitudes are derailing sound clinical judgment and treatment, professional counselors and other clinical professionals are able to ethically direct therapy. Presenting fact-based evidence, Chapter 5 provides clear insights into the types of issues people who practice BDSM are likely to present.

Being able to discern domestic violence/abuse from BDSM is at the heart of difficult and highly valid concerns expressed by people who attend the authors' workshops. In Chapter 6 key differences between domestic violence, abuse, and consensual BDSM are explored. The authors go further to explore similarly difficult and confounding issues like the relationship between self-harm and masochism, codependency, and pornography.

Previously, very little has been written about the transformative and therapeutic aspects of pain- or authority-based relationships. Using ethnographic reports, Chapter 7 addresses the efficacious limits of mainstream psychotherapeutic paradigms applied to nontraditional relationship structures by exploring, challenging, and stretching existing social and psychological dictums commonly used in clinical practice.

Overarching objectives in *Becoming a Kink Aware Therapist* are designed to

1 explore both the historical development of pathologized sexuality;
2 define healthy sexuality;
3 provide a brief overview and a clear definition of BDSM as an alternative sexual and/or relationship expression, along with descriptions of various common practices;
4 explore and clarify aspects of healthy BDSM relationships;
5 present relevant clinical research and encourage future research; and
6 offer clinical guidelines and recommendations for effective therapy.

Readers left with additional questions can gain a deeper understanding in the reference list and are encouraged to contact the authors for consultations and workshops.

Becoming a Kink Aware Therapist is a culmination of the authors' professional clinical experiences working in various modalities and multiple theoretical perspectives. The facts and aforementioned experiences are drawn from their research and work with people who represent the BDSM community. Personal and identifying characteristics have been removed from the presenting case studies to protect the anonymity of the individuals.

1 Reimagining Healthy Sexuality

"All things are subject to interpretation. Whichever interpretation prevails at a given time is a function of power and not truth."

Friedrich Nietzsche, 1967

The concept of healthy sexuality has always been culturally defined by groups and individuals with the strongest overarching social influence. The lay public construct notions of healthy sexuality by sociocultural and financial influences. Moviegoers of all ages are bombarded by common storylines enacted by idolized actresses like Julia Roberts in *Pretty Woman*, or *Cinderella* and *Sleeping Beauty*. Professional groups have also used marketing strategies to leverage panic and anxiety as motivating forces to get urgent treatment for unfounded 'disorders' like sex addiction. This chapter will highlight the historical underpinnings leading to social and professional concepts of healthy sexuality.

Pathologizing Sexuality

Richard von Krafft-Ebbing was a German psychiatrist who advocated a medical model of classification for alternative sexualities in his book *Psychopathia Sexualis: Eine Klinisch-Forensische Studie* (Sexual Psychopathy: A Clinical-Forensic Study), published in 1886. He cited case histories primarily concerning non-consensual sexual violence, which have no resemblance to what is now referred to as consensual sadomasochism or SM. Krafft-Ebbing was Sigmund Freud's inspiration for developing a system of classification of pathology, of which Freud said, "sadomasochism was the most perverse" (Freud & Strachey, 1975). The ambitious Freud knew that by setting up his pathology classification, his theories would get co-opted into legal fields.

Freud's legacy of pathologizing non-normative sexualities continues to this day. Until recently, research has been biased in that hypothetical foundations seek pathology and are non-ethnographically and nonempirically based. Freud's misinformed classifications, as they pertain to modern-day BDSM, live on in the *Diagnostic and Statistical Manual of Mental Disorders* (DSM). Over time, these definitions have become central to informing legal opinions and attitudes that lead to social, political, and cultural discrimination and persecution. In the clinical setting, this dynamic results in misdiagnosis due to demonizing what is unknown, feared, and misunderstood.

Until recently, homosexuality was an example of this form of institutionalized sociocultural pathological construction. In 1973, as a result of community organization and political activism, the gay community successfully had the classification of homosexuality removed from the DSM-III (American Psychiatric Association, 1987). This led to de-pathologizing and decriminalization of homosexuality and the cascade of dramatic social shifts we still experience in today's postmodern cultural and political discourse. This change also initiated an ongoing, large-scale process of acceptance of homosexuality as a legitimate expression of sexuality, and is now considered a cultural identity as well as a sexual orientation (Bayer, 1987; Drescher & Merlino, 2007). However, the other paraphilias continue to remain in DSM-5, largely without any unbiased clinically scientific evidence to support these expressions being pathological.

Healthy Sexuality Defined

If healthy sexuality is defined by those with the most influential voice in society, then who are they and how are they defining healthy sexuality in the current postmodern technological age? Healthy sexuality is changing as social and cultural awareness becomes open to new ideas. This prolific exposure occurs through the arts, media, and, in particular, the Internet. As a result, hidden and marginalized members of the BDSM communities are increasingly becoming more public. These social changes are preceding research and affecting the practice of psychotherapy – in particular, understanding definitions of healthy sexuality pertaining to emerging alternative sexualities.

Currently, there are no comprehensive and clear definitions of healthy sexuality that encompass emerging sexualities, particularly when addressing clients who identify with the BDSM lifestyle. The closest applicable definition was developed by the World Health Organization (WHO) in conjunction with the Pan American Health Organization (PAHO) in 2006 and then partially updated in 2010.

Sexual health: "a state of physical, emotional, mental and social well-being in relation to sexuality; it is not merely the absence of disease, dysfunction or infirmity. Sexual health requires a positive and respectful approach to sexuality and sexual relationships, as well as the possibility of having pleasurable and safe sexual experiences, free of coercion, discrimination and violence. For sexual health to be attained and maintained, the sexual rights of all persons must be respected, protected and fulfilled." (World Health Organization, 2006)

Sexuality: "a central aspect of being human throughout life encompasses sex, gender identities and roles, sexual orientation, eroticism, pleasure, intimacy and reproduction. Sexuality is experienced and expressed in thoughts, fantasies, desires, beliefs, attitudes, values, behaviors, practices, roles and relationships. While sexuality can include all of these dimensions, not all of them are always experienced or expressed. Sexuality is influenced by the interaction of biological, psychological, social, economic, political, cultural, legal, historical, religious and spiritual factors." (World Health Organization, 2006)

It is essential to point out – and very obviously clear – that these definitions are largely addressing body integrity, safety, eroticism, gender, sexual orientation, emotional attachment, and reproduction from a public health perspective, in relation to broad cultures and specific scenarios around the world.

Various authors have contrasted sexual health with sexual well-being. Sexual well-being is constructed by an individual's subjective assessment of their psychological well-being, which utilizes either a balance between positive and negative feelings pertaining to their sexual life or a favorable comparative assessment of their current sexual life with their ideal sexual life (Byers & Rehmann, 2014). Therefore, sexual health differs from sexual well-being in that the former is a broader concept. The later involves a subjective assessment of various aspects of the person's sexual relationship and functioning, satisfaction with their responsiveness, frequency of activity, and sexual repertoire.

Sexual Health	Sexuality
"a state **of physical, emotional, mental and social well-being** in relation to sexuality;	"a central aspect of being human throughout life encompasses sex, gender identities and roles, sexual orientation, eroticism, pleasure, intimacy and reproduction.
it is not merely the absence of disease, dysfunction or infirmity.	Sexuality is experienced and expressed in thoughts, fantasies, desires, beliefs, attitudes, values, behaviors, practices, roles and relationships.
Sexual health requires a **positive and respectful approach** to sexuality and sexual relationships, as well as the possibility of having pleasurable and safe sexual experiences, **free of coercion, discrimination and violence**.	While sexuality can include all of these dimensions, not all of them are always experienced or expressed.
For sexual health to be attained and maintained, the **sexual rights of all** persons must be **respected, protected and fulfilled**."	Sexuality is influenced by the interaction of biological, psychological, social, economic, political, cultural, legal, historical, religious and spiritual factors."

Figure 1.1 WHO definition of healthy sexuality.

Source: *World Health Organization, 2006*

2 There Are More Than Fifty Shades of BDSM

> "One can say that S&M is the eroticisation of power, the eroticisation of strategic relations ... the S&M game is very interesting because it is a strategic relation, because it is always fluid."
>
> – Michel Foucault (in an interview given to the *Advocate* [Gallagher & Wilson, 1984])

BDSM is an emerging phenomenon in mainstream society and, according to ethnographic research, is significantly misrepresented in the media (Ortmann & Sprott, 2013; Taylor & Ussher, 2001). The publication of E. L. James's novel *Fifty Shades of Grey* (2011) is one example of how unreliable sources lead to profound confusion and controversy within professional communities. Hollywood's rendition of BDSM as scandalous titillation precedes public and professional understanding of what this alternative sexual expression truly entails (Allen, 2013). BDSM is also more likely to be misunderstood and pathologized by behavioral health professions. In particular, professional psychotherapists have contributed to the perpetuation of stereotypes by codifying uninformed personal bias and opinions into interventions purported to be therapeutic for this population. This codifying process is very similar to the historical interventions and treatments for people who are homosexual.

What Is BDSM?

The term 'BDSM' is an abbreviation that stands for a variety of concepts and consensual behaviors enacted within a particular relationship dynamic (Magliano, 2015). The term itself dates back to 1969 (Partridge et al., 2006). Within its wide range of expressions, activities, and definitions, BDSM also includes 'kink,' a broad colloquial term for non-normative sexual behavior.[1] The general behaviors referenced here may include fetishistic interests, which may include wearing rubber, animal role-play ("furries," "dressage," puppy play), leather-sex culture and age play ("littles," Daddy/girl or Daddy/boy), to name just a few (Bean, 1994; Hébert & Weaver, 2015; Miller & Devon, 1995; Taormino, 2012; Taylor & Ussher, 2001; Williams, 2006; Wiseman, 1996). Given the aforementioned scope and focus of this handbook, it is not possible to thoroughly outline all categories, subcategories, and scenarios within these specific lifestyles and fetishes. To do so would be voluminous. The most general, overarching and essential concepts will be presented and explored in relation to BDSM, its practice and practitioners. For a more in-depth and broad look at BDSM categories readers are referred to the reference list as well as *Sexual Outsiders* by Ortmann and Sprott (2013).

- The 'B' and 'D' traditionally stands for bondage and discipline, which include activities related to restraining and inflicting extreme sensations in the form of punishment.
- The 'D' and 'S' stands for Dominance and submission and pertain to the psychological aspects of control in which one person gives the orders and the other complies. This often takes place with a written social contract. This contract may outline protocols, expectations, limits, and boundaries.
- The 'S' and 'M' stands for sadism and masochism, usually simply known and written as "SM."[2] In the media and as part of scintillating titillation, the most vivid images of BDSM relate to inflicting and receiving intense sensation, like pain. In actuality, this may not necessarily be a part of any BDSM relationship.
- Finally, the 'M' and 'S' stands for Master and slave.[3] This relates to a relationship dynamic between two consenting adults where one assumes varying degrees of authority and responsibility over a willing partner.

Strength of identification and affiliation with a common BDSM community and frequency of practice are primary determining factors that differentiate one who is curious or a fetishist from one who considers this as a part of their personal and/or sexual identity.

BDSM Practices

Consent is one of the most essential hallmarks of ethical BDSM practice (Barker, 2013; Fulkerson, 2010; Langdridge & Barker, 2007; Surprise, 2012). When adequate informed consent (permission) is provided, it is assumed that the practitioners understand the expected (intended) and potentially unexpected (unintended) outcomes of the BDSM activity or behavior that will be engaged in by the couple. Therefore, adequate consent is provided only when practitioners understand all known risks associated with the activity. Consent continues to remain even after unintended or unexpected outcomes

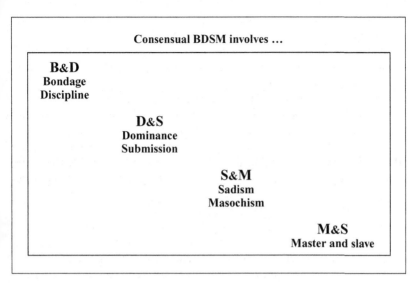

Figure 2.1 Defining what the acronyms mean in consensual BDSM.

that could not have been known when consent was initially provided. Clearly stated, consent is not retracted because of an unpredicted outcome.

The activities represented by BDSM fall along a continuum ranging from egalitarian sensation play, represented on the left in our chart, to total authority exchange (which may or may not include sensation play or fetishistic activities) on the right (Hébert & Weaver, 2015; Midori, 2005; Moser, 2006; Newmahr, 2010; Rubel & Fairfield, 2014, 2015; Taylor & Ussher, 2001). Total authority exchange is also referred to as "consensual non-consent" or "total power exchange" (TPE).[4] Authority exchange in general is also sometimes referred to as a "power dynamic relationship" or "power dynamic." This relationship dynamic may last for a few hours during a scene, or as extensively as a full-time day-to-day discipline, and may involve a complex social and emotional contract (see BDSM Relationships section below for more discussion on this). On the sensation end of this continuum, there are a huge variety of physical activities that comprise BDSM and do not necessarily involve pain experiences (Turley et al., 2011). As one moves to the right along this continuum, there is an increase in the mental and emotional control one person exercises over another (Stein et al., 2009).

Physical activities included in BDSM practices may include bondage, percussive practices, penetration, and obedience and/or service to a "Master/Mistress" or dominant partner. These physical BDSM practices require great skill and knowledge, making each activity a unique "craft" that must be learned, honed, and developed so it can be practiced safely and without permanent damage or unintended consequences.[5] Many classes and events are held across the country by BDSM support groups who teach these skills.

SM always involves negotiations regarding each partner's limits and safety. "Safe words" are used to quickly communicate boundaries and the masochist's or submissive's capacity for the specific activity being engaged in with the sadist or Dominant (Langdridge & Barker, 2007; Warren, 1998).[6] Safe words can be used to stop any activity that goes near or beyond one's negotiated limits or capacity. When BDSM practitioners engage in SM they often refer to it as 'playing' or having a 'scene.'[7] Some scenes are done in private, while some prefer public spaces (i.e., 'dungeons' at BDSM clubs or parties), either for reasons of exhibitionism or for safety when playing with a new and potentially unknown partner.

Toward the authority exchange end of the continuum, the practices involve increasing emotional, mental, and even spiritual activities (Harrington, 2011). Some people choose to exercise authority exchange dynamics for short periods of negotiated time, while others choose to live in such dynamics full-time. Non-physical BDSM activities performed to reinforce authority exchange may include obedience to one's dominant in relation to one's dress, language, behavior, and other activities (Masters, 2009; Rubel & Fairfield, 2015). Actions providing 'service'[8] are often included. Contrary to popular belief, this does not necessarily involve sexual service, although it might. Often 'service' is defined as anything that the dominant partner requests that is meaningful within the dynamics of each pair and each person's competencies and capabilities. The scope of obedience[9] is usually determined over a lengthy period of time (Rinella & Bean, 1994; Warren, 1998).

BDSM Relationships

The terms used to describe various BDSM relationships are dependent upon the communities in which they are being used (Cross & Matheson, 2006; Ortmann & Sprott, 2013; Weinberg, 1987). The distinctions among these terms, in some cases, are very blurry. The way people define their BDSM relationship depends on where they place themselves on the aforementioned continuum or a mixed combination of the two ends.

On the sensation end – the left side of our chart – practitioners identify themselves as a sadist/masochist or top/bottom. These terms primarily refer to relationships where one partner is the giver of sensation and the other partner is the receiver of physical sensation. However, to confuse things further, in the gay leather community, top and bottom may also refer to the active and receptive partner, respectively in sexual penetration (Mains, 1984). Again, it is important for clinicians to discern the client's affiliation (or lack thereof)

What do BDSMers do?		
Activities that are:	• **BONDAGE**	• **CONSCIOUSLY**
	• Rope	engage in
	• Leather	**CONSENSUALLY**
	• Chains	**AUTHORITY**
CONSCIOUS	• Sensory deprivation	**IMBALANCED**
	• **PERCUSSIVE**	relationships
	PRACTICES	• **Physical BDSM**
CONSENSUAL	• Spanking	**REQUIRES**
	• Caning	**GREAT SKILL &**
	• Flogging/whipping	**KNOWLEDGE**
Involve	• Body punching	each activity a
CONTROL &	• **PENETRATION**	unique "craft"
SURRENDER	• Piercing	• **Some BDSMers**
OF CONTROL	• Fisting	"play" in private,
	• **SENSATION PLAY**	some in public play
	• Hot wax	spaces
	• CBT	• **Negotiated limits**
	• Electricity	**SAFEWORDS**
	• **OBEY & SERVE**	
	• Follow orders	
	• Maintain	

Figure 2.2 What people who practice BDSM do.

Copyright: Shahbaz Chirinos 2016

with any specific community when using these terms. For people at this end, activities are focused on satisfying a fetish, and/or intensifying sexuality and physicality during erotic encounters. These relationships may last for one scene, or evolve into a relationship in which the pair come together only for the purposes of acting out some form of physical sensation, or people in an existing long-term relationship may identify this way. "Switches" are people who sometimes switch the role they play in BDSM activities.

Typically, relationships defined as Dominant and submissive (further to the right of the sensation continuum on our chart) incorporate or have a higher emphasis on mental control by the Dominant partner over a submissive partner (Masters, 2009; Moser & Kleinplatz, 2006). At the extreme end of this continuum, there are people in relationships who define themselves as Master and slave (M/s) (Dancer et al., 2006). This type of relationship dynamic involves a consensually agreed upon authority transfer by the slave focused on obedience and service to the Master, where the Master takes total or near-total responsibility for the slave. The M/s relationship may or may not involve physical aspects of BDSM. M/s practitioners often consider it to be part of their identity. For some the terms are relational, like 'husband' or 'wife,' meaning that they will not take on the label without a partner. Others experience being a Master or a slave as a state of being, and will keep the label even when not in an authority exchange relationship. Some people who identify in this way may live in this lifestyle full-time, others part-time (Turley et al., 2011).

Misconceptions

One of the biggest misconceptions about the terms and lifestyles of BDSM is the false belief that slaves are submissive 'doormats' to their Master (Baumeister & Butler, 1997; Kleinplatz & Moser, 2006; Masters, 2009). Some slaves are very dominant in their lives, employed in positions of decision-making and authority. People who seek to be the submissive partner in a relationship can be driven by a strong need to serve, and simply choose to be obedient; or they seek the feeling of being controlled because it gives them emotional satisfaction. A desire to be on either side of this pairing is not confined to any specific types of personality, or genders, for that matter. It is important to note that there are no one-sided generalizations about those who desire to be submissive. There are men as well as women who choose to be submissive. Often male submissives experience enormous prejudice from within the community about their choice. Some submissives desire control while others are more service oriented. It is also important to note that not all submissive types are masochists. In working with people in therapy it is wise to explore the nature of their submissiveness, the degree and nature of control or service orientation they are attracted to.

Equally, misconceptions exist in relation to dominants (Califia, 2001; Rinella & Bean, 1994; Turley et al., 2011; Warren, 1998). The largest misconception about dominants is they are arrogant, power-hungry, domineering, and usually male. Again, there are just as many males as there are women who identify as dominant. Poor psychological research combined with feminist ideologies contribute to prejudices that dominance and seeking power is unhealthy and even pathological. People seeking power or dominance can be driven by excellence, and express extreme responsibility (Shahbaz, 2012b). In a therapeutic situation, the key to working with people who identify as dominant is to explore their own understanding, construction, and expression of dominance.

It is important to note, Dominant/submissive and Master/slave are not interchangeable; they are separate definitions (Langdridge, 2006; Rubel & Fairfield, 2014). 'BDSM relationship' is not automatically synonymous with full-time authority exchange. In some geographic regions, 'BDSM relationship' can also mean – and does for the majority of people who would use that term – an egalitarian play relationship in which authority exchange is confined to sexual encounters and kept behind closed doors in the bedroom; that is, part of sexual repertoire and/or fantasy between consenting couples. Furthermore, depending on people's sexual orientation, different terms are applied to describe relationships (Ortmann & Sprott, 2013; Taylor & Ussher, 2001). In the heterosexual communities, terms like BDSM, Dominance and submission, and Master slave are more commonly used than in the gay leather community. The gay leather community will use terms like 'top' and 'bottom' to describe not only sexual preference, but also relationship dynamic of who is dominant or submissive. The nuances of definitions may be specific to a region, community, or sub community. Psychotherapists need to be informed of these nuanced differences.

It is also important to highlight that masochism has been conflated with pathological self-harm (Ross, 2012). The unquestioned psychopathologizing of masochism has automatically led to the stigmatization of any behavior related to intense sensations as enjoyment. Similarly, sadism has been misunderstood as a perversion and dangerous, instead of an expression (Bienvenu, 1998; Langdridge, 2006; Langdridge & Barker, 2007). It has been demonized with violence, conflated with patriarchy and criminality.

Altered States of Consciousness

Not all aspects of BDSM are rooted in sex. BDSM also provides a means of attaining altered states of consciousness for some practitioners, and has been reported by them as being spiritual in some way (Beckmann, 2008; Harrington, 2011). Practices such as controlled pain, emotional discipline, and devotion

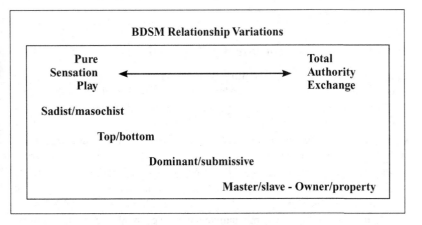

Figure 2.3 Relationship variations in consensual BDSM.

Copyright: Shahbaz Chirinos 2016

have been used for centuries as means to access altered states of consciousness, spiritual evolution, development, and enlightenment. Throughout all
time and all cultures there has been a place for those individuals seeking
the path of obedience, devotion and service to a higher spiritual power. The
more physical aspects of these practices are present in Native American traditions (Lakota Sun Dance), Sufi and Hindu (Kavadi ritual) practices, and
even in Christianity (crucifixions and penances) (Glucklich, 2001). These
practices are referred to colloquially as the "Ordeal Path" (Kaldera, 2006). In
indigenous societies, these have involved culturally specific acts of devotion,
surrender, and sacrifice, and elaborate rituals involving specific garments
and objects that have strong symbolic meaning for those peoples. In many
instances, community involvement is provided through prayer, preparation,
and post-ceremonial caregiving. Many indigenous practitioners experience
an altered state of consciousness and report spiritual experiences that are, at
best, difficult to describe (Glucklich, 2001). We conjecture that pairing this
experience to extreme physical stress concurrent with community witnessing
is transformative and bonding from a tribal non-individualistic perspective.

Similar experiences are described by people practicing BDSM (Ambler
et al., in press; Harrington, 2011; Kaldera, 2006; Lee et al., 2016; Sagarin
et al., 2015). On a physical level, all involved experience altered states of
consciousness, often referred to as 'subspace' or 'Domspace,'[10] during scenes
within the BDSM culture and practice. Feelings of intense love, devotion,
gratitude, and ego surrender are frequently reported by SM practitioners, as
well as 'leaving the body' and spiritual communing with perceived higher
powers. Some deliberately use SM techniques as a transformative and spiritual
path. Chapter 3 further expands on the research on the psycho-neuro-biology
involved in the practice of BDSM.

BDSM Culture: Role of Ritual and Symbolism

BDSM is a multidimensional culture with its own set of rituals and symbolism
(Beckmann, 2008; Mains, 1984; Martin et al., 2011; Rubel, 2008; Shahbaz,
2008). Similar to the cultural communities mentioned above, objects incorporated into community rituals are meaningful symbols. Likewise, BDSM
communities also incorporate symbolic articles, which also convey strong
meaning to community members. These rituals and symbols will vary from
community to community, so it is best not to assume that any one symbol
or ritual is meaningful to a client until you have discerned their community
involvement (or lack of it).

Clothing is one of the key mechanisms to convey symbolic and metaphorical significance within some BDSM communities, as the choice and type
of clothing can be an integral part of the emotional and mental obedience

and control aspect of some BDSM relationships (Baldwin, 2002; Easton & Liszt, 2000; Martin et al., 2011; Ortmann & Sprott, 2013; Weinberg, 2006). Certain clothing or jewelry may be used to signify whether someone is in a submissive or dominant mode. For example, in "Leather" communities, a Master's "cover" (usually a Muir cap) is generally worn only by a person who has been deemed qualified as a full-time respected Master by his or her peers (Bean, 1994). Traditionally, a Master's cap is given to him/her in a community ritual setting to denote that they are responsible and ethical in their dominant authority exchange practices.

However, it is important to note that not all BDSM communities incorporate leather principles. In different parts of North America, BDSM, Master slave, and Leather communities may be segregated (Levine & Shahbaz, 2010). This is also true across Europe, England, and Australia (Shahbaz, 2009b). In working with individuals in therapy, explore how they express, understand, or give meaning to the various rituals and symbols in their practice of BDSM (Chirinos, 2015; Levine & Shahbaz, 2010).

In some communities, a 'collar' signifies someone is in service or 'owned' by another person as a submissive, slave, or bottom; in others, it can be simply a fashion statement, possibly indicating that one is kinky, and the meaning should be determined before making assumptions. In some M/s relationships, slaves undergo a series of trials that test their commitment of service to their master, as well as the various aspects of the specific type of lifestyle they are willing to be involved in. The consolidation of this commitment and depth of understanding is typically done within a collaring ritual. This is usually a private ceremony held with community or lifestyle members as witnesses (Easton & Liszt, 2000; Levine & Shahbaz, 2010; Rubel & Wiseman, 2006; Townsend, 1993). There are various types of collars ranging from leather to chain and metal; collars can be as blatant as a dog collar from the pet store or as subtle as an attractive necklace or wristband. Each signifies a different subculture a person may identify with. Typically, people who choose chain collars are associated with the Leather culture, particularly the gay Leather subculture, while those who wear leather or metal collars are associated with pansexual[11] subcultures.

Black leather has also come to symbolize, for many people, what mainstream society mentally, emotionally, sexually, and psychologically suppress. Robert Bienvenu drew the historic association among BDSM, homosexuality, and biker culture (Bienvenu, 1998). Much of the significance of this symbolism is historically related to the biker culture post World War II. Groups of returned servicemen formed motorcycle groups and developed comradeship. Some of these groups were clandestine because of their homosexual nature. These underground expressions of hyper-masculinity borrowed many rituals and symbols from the general biker culture and now is historically been referred to as 'old guard' (Townsend, 1993). Thus, symbols and images of BDSM became associated with hyper-masculinity, particularly within the gay leather subcultures (Rambukkana, 2007). While many arguments prevail in mainstream BDSM communities about whether 'old guard' actually existed, it highlights many symbolic associations about sexuality and masculinity.

Leather gives permission to express the dark side of the human self within a currently emerging alternative culture. BDSM and Leather cultures provide a metaphorical 'container' to explore the unspoken and avoided darker aspects of one's humanity through conscious intention and reflection, in a safe and heavily structured space (Moore, 1990; Ramsour, 2002; Shahbaz, 2008, 2009a, 2010).

In Leather subcultures, the practice of 'earning leather' distantly echoes indigenous rites of passage (Baldwin & Bean, 1993; Sisson, 2007; Townsend, 1993; Weinberg, 2006). Articles of leather clothing are gifted to people who are seen to have served their community by passing on skills, doing honorable deeds, providing 'service,' or for supporting and building their community. Leather items are bestowed either by one's Master, or by peers in the community, either publicly or privately.

Another example of symbolism within the BDSM subcultures involves the multilayered symbolism of leather. Black leather clothing symbolically signifies the dark side of one's personality, which is part of all human nature. Carl Jung described this as "the Shadow" (Jung, 1953). He pointed out a personal as well as collective shadow. The shadow is by its very nature unconscious, and therefore difficult to address; many psychotherapists rarely, if ever, address this shadow aspect of personal and interpersonal relationships and identity (Abrams & Zweig, 1991). The various practices, rituals, and symbols associated with BDSM consciously engage with the individual shadow. Traditionally, psychotherapists are not trained to identify or work with shadow elements in their clinical work.[12] Mainstream therapists are trained to explore cognitive behavioral aspects of presenting problems, most notably psychiatric disorders. They lack the theoretical frameworks or skills to unpack the symbolic and archetypal metaphors coded in their client's stories. Clinical practice fails to explore the mythic connections or unravel deeper unconscious layers of meanings in what appears to be obvious from an analytic perspective. Thus, many psychotherapists miss rich and deep psychological opportunities to help their clients delve into and explore hidden, suppressed, or repressed elements of themselves.

Community building and developing strong community bonds, networks, and support is extremely important for this marginalized group (Bienvenu, 1998; Holt, 2016; Kleinplatz & Moser, 2006; Mains, 1984; Ortmann & Sprott, 2013; Shahbaz, 2009b, 2010). These rituals and ceremonies concretize acceptance of an individual within an alternative community. This acceptance of one's identity and alternative interests is the inverse of the experience the members have with mainstream society.

Defining Healthy BDSM Relationships

BDSM communities and their various subcultures define healthy BDSM relationships as, first and foremost, involving uncoerced consent, given free from emotional blackmail or manipulation by either party. The amount of authority and control granted and accepted is determined and negotiated by each pair, reflecting their individual core values, principles, and community involvement.

Core values generally considered by many BDSM communities to nourish healthy relationships include honor, mutual respect, integrity, and responsibility. Healthy BDSM relationships demonstrate trust, caring, and an ongoing commitment to mutual growth, which are all valid indicators of any positive mainstream relationship. Therapists may want to explore the degree of congruence between people's values and their actions. To what extent do people do what they say or believe in?

Certain principles prescribed by the larger BDSM community guide what are considered to be healthy behaviors or actions. These include values and actions focused on behaving in ways that are "Safe, Sane, and Consensual" (SSC), or alternately, with "Risk-Aware Consensual Kink" (RACK) and more recently, "Caring, Communication, Consent, and Caution" (4Cs) (Williams et al., 2014). In more tightly knit communities, the actions of the dominant and submissive are reflective of the individual's understanding and degree of devotion to the lifestyle and his or her partner.

Community support is essential to healthy BDSM relationships, if only to combat shame and learn safe SM techniques. To that end, BDSM communities devote a great deal of time and effort to hold meetings, educational workshops, and community forums for people to engage, build community, and find support with one another.

These core values, principles, and social frameworks all indicate the practice of BDSM operates in its own valid cultural construct and context. As such, SSC is defined in context of the individuals in the relationship. Generally speaking, safety involves not inflicting permanent damage or unexpected/unintended outcomes. This involves the participants knowing the limits of their capabilities with any given technique. The definition of sanity within this cultural context references behavior as judged from the norms within the specific BDSM cultural group in which the behaviors are taking place. Sanity is defined while members of this group are fully and clinically orientated and aware of the real and potential impact of the participant's decisions.

In addition to the above, the authors recommend exploring an individual's sense of inner well-being as an important aspect of determining the health of their BDSM practices. It is also important to determine whether your client's interest in BDSM is a matter of identity (i.e., do they define themselves as Master, slave, etc.), or only one aspect of their sexual exploration and repertoire. This determines how important BDSM activities are to the people involved and the extent they are willing/able to bracket these activities within their lives. We also recommend exploring the nature and quality of supportive communication process a couple in a BDSM relationships have implemented – in particular, communication processes for constructively dealing with conflict or problems.

Also, because of the nature of sociopolitical pathologizing that occurs toward sexually marginalized communities, it is important for therapists to ascertain whether clients who are BDSM practitioners have supportive infrastructure. The extent to which people have connected to culturally supportive networks and community around them is a very important aspect of building healthy BDSM communities and one's personal identity as a BDSM participant.

Having said that, it is important to note, many people choose not to seek out communities. There are many reasons for this. Some people may be ashamed of their sexual interests. Seeking out and belonging to a specific community would require an overt, somewhat public, and conscious affirmation of these alternative interests. Others may be afraid of rejection. This fear of rejection may include anxieties related to self-judgments – fear of not being 'good' enough. These anxieties may entail being perceived as not being masochistic enough, 'submissive' enough, or 'dominant' enough as defined by the specific community one wishes to belong. On the other hand, perhaps they have tried to reach out to others but found local communities lacking or not aligned to their interests. Some people are afraid of being recognized, preferring to remain anonymous. Finding community is more than sharing similar sexual kinks. Community, by definition, needs to support a sense of being intellectually and socioeconomically similarly minded.

Table 2.1 Summary of Key Areas in the Shahbaz-Chirinos Healthy BDSM Checklist

Shahbaz-Chirinos Healthy BDSM Behavior Checklist	
Key Area	*What to Explore*
Consent	*Check to verify your clients engage in BDSM consensually. Clarify if their definition of consent includes known and unknown or potentially unexpected outcomes and incorporates an understanding of their skills in specific activities.*

Shahbaz-Chirinos Healthy BDSM Behavior Checklist

Key Area	What to Explore
Wellness	Ask questions related to their sense of inner well-being. Does the person feel a sense of expansion and well-being, broadly and specifically, as a result of engaging in BDSM?
Values	Ask questions to determine the existence of your client's culturally appropriate values; i.e. honor, integrity, responsibility, SSC and RACK. Is there incongruence between these values and what and how they engage in BDSM?
Walking the talk	Value/Action Congruence. Ask questions about their values and see if they are congruent with the behavioral dynamics of the relationship.
Clarity	Ask questions related to the client's purpose, vision or philosophy about their relationship.
Identity	Ask questions to determine if BDSM is part of their sexual identity or just one aspect of their sexual exploration and repertoire.
Skills & knowledge	Ask questions to discern whether they have developed culturally appropriate knowledge and skills about the practical application of BDSM practices.
Supportive networks[1]	Check to see if they have built culturally appropriate and consistent micro-systems and infrastructure to support their relationship choices; i.e. educational and social groups.
Dyadic problem solving processes	Check to see if they have developed culturally appropriate and consistent communication processes, especially around problem solving, which support their relationship choices.
Supportive community	Determine if they are connected to a larger BDSM community for support. And, if not, explore reasons for lack of connection and involvement.

1 Supportive networks differ from supportive communities in that the former are micro systems (i.e. mentors, individuals, close relationships). The latter refers to larger communities (regional groups, membership within groups, clubs, international associations and clubs).

In keeping with these guidelines, the authors have developed a checklist for psychotherapists to assist them in evaluating healthy BDSM behavior in clients.

Domestic violence will be explored in depth and contrasted with consensual BDSM in Chapter 6.

Notes

1 Non-normative sexual behavior is behavior that violates commonly held overt cultural and social standards, including morals and belief systems within a specific or larger community or population, which are relative to the time in which the behavior is expressed or engaged in.

2 SM is also written as S/m.

3 Master slave can be denoted as M/s or Ms.

4 Total power exchange is considered by some to be an inaccurate philosophical representation of BDSM relationship dynamics. The authors contend that "Total Authority Exchange" is a more accurate term, since it encompasses the notion that one person willingly surrenders complete authority to another. Total authority exchange usually involves long-term relationships. These interactions are not common and not quickly entered into as they involve complete trust and respect. There is, ideally, a high level of ethical philosophy and responsibility on the part of the person assuming total authority. Power is retained regardless if authority is relinquished.

5 Fully informed and adequate consent also incorporates the consideration of one's skills, abilities, and limits, psychologically, mentally, and physically, continuously and at any specifically given point in time.

6 In this text "Dominant" will be capitalized when referring to one's identity expression or title; "dominant" will be lowercase when referring to one's personal characteristic.

7 The authors prefer the term "scene" over "play," as the later implies a lack of serious and methodical consideration with BDSM engagement. For purposes of this book, "scene" will be used in lieu of "play."

8 Service is a culturally defined voluntary act either within one's dominant/submissive relationship or to a larger community. In the first case, it is a voluntary action in response to one's dominant partner's requests; in the second case, it promotes community building. It is usually an act that is performed willingly, often based on devotion. Concrete examples include volunteering time and/or special skills, and teaching or mentoring work within one's chosen community.

9 Obedience is defined as compliance with the dominant's protocol, desires, or directives. It may, however, may have more specific philosophical and pragmatic implications that are unique to the specific couple.

10 "Subspace" for submissives or bottoms and "Domspace" or "Topspace" for Dominants or Masters are terms used describe an altered state of consciousness as a result of engaging in BDSM. Sagarin et. al. (2015) describes this experience as subjectively pleasant and blissed-out for the submissives or bottoms and feelings of a driven, all-powerful euphoric feeling for tops or Dominants.

11 The term 'pansexual' is used for someone whose attraction is not limited by gender (biological sex), gender expression, or sexual orientation. 'Pan' is Greek for 'all.' Individuals who identify as pansexual do not have sex with animals.

12 The Council for Accreditation of Counseling & Related Educational Programs 2016 Standards can be found at http://www.cacrep.org/for-programs/2016-cacrep-standards/.

3 Is It "Bad," "Mad," and "Sick" or, Is It Okay?

> *"Through the various discourses, legal sanctions against minor perversions were multiplied; sexual irregularity was annexed to mental illness; from childhood to old age, a norm of sexual development was defined and all the possible deviations were carefully described; pedagogical controls and medical treatments were organized; around the least fantasies, moralists, but especially doctors, brandished the whole emphatic vocabulary of abomination."*
>
> – Michel Foucault, 1978

In 2005, Margie Nichols wrote, "in many ways the BDSM community of the early 21st century resembles the gay community of the 1970s, and individuals who struggle with BDSM desires experience a similar internalized shame about their sexuality" (2005, p. 292). However, the general and professional population unwittingly accept the media's depiction of alternative sexualities as fact without critical analysis or accurate information. This acceptance may commonly occur because it validates therapist's own normative views about sexuality and sexual expression (Kolmes et al., 2006; Powers, 2007; Van Der Walt, 2014).

The impact of bias, in the form of 'kinkophobia' (see Chapter 4), has led to traditional research being based entirely on pathological paradigms (Shahbaz, 2012a). As previously mentioned, Krafft-Ebing's and Freud's legacies have led to persistent misconceptions about individuals who engage in these practices. These misconceptions have become codified as pathology in the DSM and have greatly influenced social misunderstanding of BDSM concepts and practice (Silverstein, 2009). Little objective academic research of value has been done in this area until fairly recently.

Starting with the use of the DSM-5 definitions for BDSM populations and their clinical implications, this chapter sets out to critically analyze and present the bio-socio-psychological research related to the practice of BDSM.

It will conclude with research into "kinkophobia" within the community of therapists and its effect on clinical practice.

DSM-5

The most recent publication of the DSM-5 in 2013 led to a liberation of the BDSM community from a long history of psychopathology (Downing, 2015; Lin, 2014; Wright, 2006, 2010). However, it also contributes to further controversy and confusion regarding this text's efficacy as an earnest psychotherapeutic tool firmly steeped in sound guiding psychological as well as clinical principles. As a result, it is important to understand the challenge of defining psychopathology and mental disorders. More essentially, psychotherapists must understand how clinical decisions have legal ramifications for their clients and, therefore, may need to work in tandem with legal professionals.

Psychopathology and Mental Disorders Defined

Maddux and Winstead (2012) in *Psychopathology: Foundations for a Contemporary Understanding* consider two definitions for the term: first as a statistical deviance, a phenomenon that lies outside of the range of normal and typical experience (i.e., statistically deviant or infrequent); and second, as maladaptive or dysfunctional behavior. Both are common sense; however, norms are established by use of psychometrics, which is dependent upon the operational (conceptual) definition used to create the measure, which in turn is used in research resulting in the establishment of group norms. Complex and abstract concepts in research are problematic in that they are difficult to quantify and measure (e.g., love, or 'normal' sexual behavior). Both definitions for psychopathology are potentially flawed in that they are subject to bias through subjectivity either in the development of the operational definition (statistical deviance) or situational context. Maladaptive behavior in one situation may not be effective in coping with stress, but the same behavior may be successful in mitigating stress in another scenario or circumstance.

In lieu of the term psychopathology, the DSM-5 uses and outlines the definition of mental disorder as follows:

> A mental disorder is a syndrome characterized by clinically significant disturbance in an individual's cognition, emotion regulation, or behavior that reflects a dysfunction in the psychological, biological, or developmental processes underlying mental functioning. Mental disorders are usually associated with significant distress or disability

in social, occupational, or other important activities. An expectable or culturally approved response to a common stressor or loss, such as the death of a loved one, is not a mental disorder. Socially deviant behavior (e.g., political, religious, or sexual) and conflicts that are primarily between the individual and society are not mental disorders unless the deviance or conflict results from a dysfunction in the individual, as described above. (American Psychiatric Association, 2013)

Determining abnormality in the form of psychopathology or a mental disorder requires clinical decision-making, which results from the incorporation of an understanding of deviation from cultural norms, personal distress, statistical infrequency, and impaired social functioning (Van Der Walt, 2014) – all of which is understood in a larger social environmental context, for example, social stigma and forensic investigations (Bezreh et al., 2012; T. O. Brown, 2010; Hoff & Sprott, 2009; Iannotti, 2014; Khan, 2009, 2014, 2015; Lin, 2014; Moulds, 2015; Pa, 2001). The DSM-5 incorporated this understanding by revisiting and correcting diagnostic errors of sexual sadism and masochism in its prior publications.

Sexual Masochism and Sadism Disorders

Sexual masochism disorder and sexual sadism disorder in the DSM-5 are grouped within the category of paraphilic disorders (Highlights of Changes from DSM-IV-TR to DSM-5).[1] It clarified that people with "atypical sexual interests" are not mentally ill as earlier editions declared; instead, it introduced a new category of disorder. A person is considered as having a disorder if

a) they experience distress beyond what's expected from the social stigmatization surrounding their atypical sexuality; and
b) it infringes on others, particularly those who are unwilling or unable to consent.

The essential changes from DSM-IV TR to DSM-5 with respect to relevant sexological disorders presented in this handbook can be reviewed on the American Psychiatric Association (APA) website as well as by the following statement from the National Coalition for Sexual Freedom.[2] Michael First writes, "DSM-5 contains numerous additions to the descriptive text for paraphilic disorders intended to provide guidance to evaluators in forensic contexts" (First, 2014, p. 197). This outlines the most essential argument that the DSM-5 has moved away from being a psychological tool for use in clinical professional settings to one supporting legal forensic prosecutions. He argues these changes result in a wider interpretation of what constitutes a formal clinical disorder rather than an unusual sexual interest (paraphilia), which is, according to the DSM-5, absent of any clinical pathology.

It is further argued that the vague and clinically undefined terms of "psychosocial difficulties" and "significant distress," pertaining only to those individuals who freely admit to having said paraphilic interests, is problematic in that it lacks precision; therefore, it remains open to legal and psychological debate (Bennett, 2013). The current version of DSM-5 further lacks a definition of harm. Paradigms used to construct the definition of harm would be useful, as it is one of several essential issues in defining consent, and particularly vexing when applied to M/s or D/s relationships.

Unlike sexual masochism disorder, the diagnostic criteria for sexual sadism disorder, per the DSM-5, pertains to both patients who either freely or unwillingly admit to having paraphilic interests involving "physical or psychological suffering of another individual despite substantial objective evidence to the contrary." The non-admitting individual's criteria shall be met, in part, "if there is corroborating evidence of a strong or preferential interest in pain and suffering involving multiple victims." This opens a door to unconfirmed and possibly maliciously motivated victim reports. There is no way to validate these reports from independent resources, nor would the subject (the accused) of the report likely have the right to challenge them. This is contrary to legal principles established in courts. How exactly does a therapist go outside the client-therapist relationship set out in the ethical standards for professional conduct to obtain such 'evidence' to rule out or rule in a paraphilic disorder? These arguments also require redefining "non-admitting individuals."

Despite these difficulties, as a result of the clarifications in the DSM-5, it is very salient to note that from 2012 to 2014 the National Coalition for Sexual Freedom (NCSF) has seen a 57.5 percent drop in requests for child custody legal assistance related to separating couples in a BDSM relationship (Wright, 2015). They attribute this drop to the following:

> Now the paraphilias are considered to be "unusual sexual interests," while those who have sex with children or people who haven't consented, or who deliberately cause harm to themselves or others, may be diagnosed with a Paraphilic Disorder. (National Coalition for Sexual Freedom[3])

BDSM Demographics

In the psychotherapeutic community, there are elements of confusion and misunderstanding related to whether these practices are fetishistic or constitute a legitimate identity or orientation (Ramsour, 2002). Although research has typically been unreliable, it is important to consider and cross-reference a number of studies.

Several recent surveys conducted in Australia and the United States indicate prevalence rates of 15 to 20 percent of surveyed participants who report engaging in BDSM at some time in their lives (Richters et al., 2003, 2008). From a national sample of 2,742 participants, Janus and Janus reported 14 percent of men and 11 percent of women in the US have had experience with BDSM (Janus & Janus, 1993). This and other studies show the percentage of people practicing BDSM to be nearly comparable to the percentage of people who identify as gay and lesbian. Psychometric comparison of BDSM practitioners compared to controls showed BDSM practitioners were less neurotic, more extraverted, more conscientious, less sensitive to rejection, had higher subjective well-being, and were more open to new experiences (T. O. Brown, 2010; Connolly, 2006; Wismeijer & Van Assen, 2013).

Additionally, the Kinsey Institute's 1990 report on sex indicated that 5 to 10 percent of the US population participates in some form of SM at least occasionally (Reinisch et al., 1990). This is an older study, therefore the percentages are likely higher today due to the role of media and social networking previously discussed. The real significance or importance of this study is in the demographics, which indicate that those who engage in BDSM represent a viable sexual minority comparable in size to the gay and lesbian community.

BDSM Prevalence

Percentage of BDSM practitioners

15–20% of participants in several surveys conducted in Australia and USA (2005; 2007) reported having engaged in BDSM at some time in their lives.

The number of folks practicing BDSM appears to be comparable to the number of folks who are gay and lesbian.

Kinsey Institute new report on sex: 5–10% of US population does some form of S/m at least occasionally

BDSM represents a sexual minority.

Figure 3.1 Prevalence of BDSM.
Copyright: Shahbaz Chirinos 2016

Debunking BDSM Myths

Many psychological models and paradigms are based on persistently misconceived theories and assumptions that presuppose healthy relationships must be constructed with equal authority (Baumeister, 1997; Kleinplatz & Moser, 2004, 2005; Ortmann & Sprott, 2013; Rodemaker, 2008). The false presumption in our society is that only individuals who are not on equal footing would enter into relationships with unequal authority structures. There is a difference between the negotiated agreements pertaining to a relationship structure and the way in which these agreements are expressed and embodied. It is possible for two people, each from a position of equality, respect, and authority, to agree to construct a relationship structure based on unequal authority. The same couple may then proceed to express themselves in the agreed constructs of unequal authority. This does not diminish their self-agency. The implementation of their agreed unequal authority has been agreed and consented to consciously. That agreement and consent was done on equal footing (Surprise, 2012). It is the authors' contention that these paradigms and assumptions have remained unchallenged for sociopolitical reasons, and therefore do not account for consensual inequality as a valid alternative for a healthy relationship. Recent research dispels many of these myths and highlights the need to directly hear the voices of members from this community. Some of those key findings include the following:

- No evidence that a BDSM orientation is caused by childhood trauma or a history of abuse (Kleinplatz & Moser; 2004; Richters et al., 2003).
- People labeled with "paraphilic sexuality" suffer discrimination and social stigmatization in the way homosexuals suffered before the changes in the DSM III in 1973 (Langdridge, 2006; Moser & Kleinplatz, 2006; Wright, 2010).
- BDSM does not cause distress and dysfunction in individuals. Sociocultural and political persecutions are most likely the cause of distress and dysfunction in individuals practicing BDSM (Moser & Kleinplatz, 2006; Richters et al., 2003).
- BDSM is a viable and healthy outlook on lifestyle and sexuality (Baumeister & Butler, 1997; Benz & Benz, 2015; Cross & Matheson, 2006; Hsu et al., 1994; Kleinplatz & Moser, 2004; Langdridge, 2006; Lawrence & Love-Crowell, 2008; Sandnabba et al., 2002; Wismeijer & Van Assen, 2013).

Empirical research does not support the notion that clients with BDSM have a greater history of past abuse or trauma that predisposes them to this form of sexual or relationship expression. In long-term BDSM relationships, there are often contracts that involve considerable negotiation and forethought. Practitioners tend to be more introspective and thoughtful regarding what

Recent Research Findings in BDSM			
Academic Research			
• Thin and sparse • Irrelevant non empirical assumptions		• Based on pathological paradigms • Not ethnographic	
Recent Research Indicates...			
No evidence that a BDSM orientation is caused by childhood trauma, or history of abuse. (Kleinplatz & Moser; 2004; Richter et al. 2008)	People labeled with Paraphilic sexuality suffer discrimination and social stigmatization in the way homosexuals suffered before the changes in 1973. (Langdridge 2006; Moser & Kleinplatz, 2006)	BDSM does not cause distress and dysfunction in individuals. Socio-cultural and political persecution most likely cause of distress and dysfunction in individuals practicing BDSM. (Moser, 2006)	BDSM is a viable and healthy outlook to lifestyle and sexuality. (Baumeister & Butler, 1997; Cross & Matheson, 2006; Hsu et al., 1994; Kleinplatz & Moser, June 2004; Langdridge 2006; Lawrence & Love-CroIll 2008; Sandnabba, Santtila, & Nordling, 2002; Linberg, 1987)

Figure 3.2 Recent research findings on BDSM.
Copyright: Shahbaz Chirinos 2016

is important to them, what they want, and what they do not want – all of which require strong, intact personal boundaries to negotiate a sexual scene related to one's fantasies. The authors' professional experience reinforces a recent finding from the National Coalition for Sexual Freedom latest survey[4] that BDSM practitioners generally tend to have a higher level of self-esteem; are healthier than the average person; have better than average communication skills, imagination, and self-awareness; and are capable of undergoing insightful reflection during psychotherapy.

Psychobiology of BDSM

Some of the most useful research in understanding the phenomenon of BDSM is coming from the field of psychobiology. Recently several researchers have been investigating the psychobiology of BDSM to understand what motivates this practice. It appears the research is reinforcing the verbal statements of practitioners in ethnographic studies. In other words, they do it because it makes them feel good.

These research findings are reinforcing practitioners' statements that, paradoxically, BDSM increases relationship closeness. These subjective reports are also supported by objective scientific measures (Ambler et al., in press; Beckmann, 2008; Sagarin et. al., 2009). In a paper recently submitted for publication entitled "Consensual BDSM facilitates role-specific altered states of consciousness," Ambler et al. support this notion and stated the following:

> Researchers studying consensual BDSM ... have theorized that individuals pursue BDSM activities, in part, due to the pleasant altered states of consciousness these activities produce. (Ambler et al., in press)

This research proposes Csíkszentmihályi and Dietrich's theory of flow and transient hypofrontality, respectively, as correlatives with practitioners' reports of altered states of consciousness typically known as 'subspace' and 'Topspace.'

Flow, as described by Mihaly Csíkszentmihályi, contains the following elements and is defined as completely focused motivation, coupled with a single-minded immersion of an act (Csíkszentmihályi, 1991).

1   Intense and focused concentration on the present moment
2   Merging of action and awareness
3   A loss of reflective self-consciousness
4   A sense of personal control or agency over the situation or activity
5   A distortion of temporal experience; one's subjective experience of time is altered
6   Experience of the activity as intrinsically rewarding, also referred to as *autotelic experience*

Dietrich's (2003) transient hypofrontality hypothesis has two essential premises:

a)   The brain has limited resources, and brain structures, systems, and areas compete for these resources.
b)   The subjective experience of consciousness is a process.

In yet another interesting study, Bert Cutler's Ph.D. dissertation investigated a group of BDSM practitioners before and after they practiced sadomasochistic acts with psychobiological measures (Cutler, 2003). His research reported participants experiencing increased closeness with each other and, most importantly, the psychobiological indices demonstrated a definite health benefit from flogging and other extreme-sensation practices: decreased levels of the stress hormone cortisol. These results were further replicated between BDSM practitioners who switched from topping to bottoming, with non-familiar partners.

In a separate study, Sagarin and his associates (2009) also reported findings that BDSM practices contribute to health benefits related to stress management, evidenced in decreased cortisol levels. They suggest the "flow" described by BDSM practitioners is similar psychobiologically to the "high" described by athletes and spiritual "peaks" meditators experience. In attempts to further explain these results, Sagarin and his team propose that BDSM may be transformative.

Social Persecution and Discrimination

People who practice BDSM are often subject to social persecution and discrimination (Klein & Moser, 2006). The forms these take vary from child custody battles, contentious divorce judgments, work-related discrimination, bullying, stalking, and blackmail – see Table 3.1, the NCSF 2014 breakdown of requests for help in incident reporting and responses, below (T. O. Brown, 2010; Iannotti, 2014; Khan, 2014; Wright, 2014, 2015). Therapists may be called as expert witnesses to reinforce or refute pathological perspectives of BDSM practice and relationships. It is important to be informed and to practice professional ethics of "do no harm."

The National Coalition for Sexual Freedoms **(NCSF)** was formed in 1997 by a small group led by Susan Wright under the auspices of the New York SM Activists. The goal was to fight for sexual freedom and privacy rights for all adults who engage in safe, sane, and consensual behavior. To defend sexual freedom rights, they are allied with the Free Speech Coalition, the American Civil Liberties Union (ACLU), the American Association of Sex Educators, Counselors and Therapists (AASECT), the Society for the Scientific Study of Sexuality (SSSS), the National Gay and Lesbian Task Force, and the Gay and Lesbian Activist Alliance, among others. NCSF's mission statement states:

> NCSF is committed to creating a political, legal and social environment in the US that advances equal rights for consenting adults who engage in alternative sexual and relationship expressions. The NCSF aims to advance the rights of, and advocate for consenting adults in the BDSM-Leather-Fetish, Swing, and Polyamory Communities. We pursue our vision through direct services, education, advocacy, and outreach, in conjunction with our partners, to directly benefit these communities.[5]

NCSF's Incident Reporting and Response (IRR) helps people who are being discriminated against because they are kinky and/or non-monogamous (Wright, 2015). In 2014, over 1,200 kinky people directly accessed NCSF's Kink-Aware Professionals (KAP) list to find a lawyer, therapist, or other professional rather than asking NCSF for help through NCSF's Incident Reporting and Response (see Wright, 2015, *NCSF's Annual Incident Reporting* in the Appendix for a summary of requests for assistance from NCSF in fighting persecution and discrimination). It is likely a greater awareness of resources available through NCSF have resulted in an increased use of the KAP referral list. From 2002 to 2011, NCSF's IRR received over 500 requests every year. In 2012, that number dropped to 474. In 2014, that number dropped even further, to 184. This change is considered to be likely due to the changes in the DSM-5 as well as an increased use of the KAP resource.

Susan Wright, NCSF's director of the IRR, documented 184 requests for help in 2014. Of the 184 requests for assistance, the majority dealt with BDSM, while only 6 involved polyamory/swing issues. Of those dealing with BDSM, apart from request for information from professionals, the top five requests related to criminal issues, child custody, kink group issues, and discrimination issues.

Table 3.1 NCSF 2014 Breakdown of Requests for Help in Incident Reporting and Responses

Rank	No. of IRR requests	Issues
1	73	criminal issues
2	33	child custody
3	26	requests for info from professionals
4	20	kink group issues
5	10	discrimination issues
6	5	job discrimination
7	6	media related incidents
8	4	divorce
9	4	civil law issues
10	3	outings

Source: Wright, S. (2015). *NCSF Incident Reporting & Response Annual Report*. Retrieved from https://ncsfreedom.org/key-programs/incident-response/incident-response.html

NCSF reports that of the 73 requests involving criminal issues, 42 were for assistance with victim services, reporting an assault, sexual assault, blackmail, or talking to the police and obtaining restraining orders; 13 were for referrals to kink-aware defense attorneys; 6 were for sex workers seeking assistance upon being arrested; another 6 dealt with assisting people who were dealing with probation, sex offenders, and sex traffickers; and 5 were for research on state criminal laws and contracts.[6] These statistics indicate the continuing prevalence of criminalizing atypical sexual behavior.

The statistics related to divorce and child custody are another indication of the lack of understanding and continued persecution through criminalization of BDSM practitioners (Klein & Moser, 2006; Wright, 2014). The importance of the depathologizing of BDSM practices as a mental illness is indicated by the significant drop in 2014 statistics for help with child custody/divorce issues, presumed to be related to the change in the DSM-5 criteria, which made it clear that people who are kinky are not mentally ill.

Table 3.2 indicates NCSF statistics demonstrate an even bigger change, which is due to the DSM-5 publication in 2013. It is plausible to interpret this dramatic decline in requests for assistance as resulting in an inverse correlation, resulting in a higher percentage of kinky parents who now retain child custody. Table 3.3 also supports this hypothesis.

Table 3.2 Number of Requests for Assistance from NCSF with Child Custody and Divorce

Year	# of requests
2009 –	132 people
2010 –	125 people
2011 –	115 people
2012 –	87 people
2013 –	Not available
2014 –	37 people
2015	30 people

Source: Modified from Wright, S. (2015). *NCSF Incident Reporting & Response Annual Report.* Retrieved from https://ncsfreedom.org/key-programs/incident-response/incident-response.html

Table 3.3 Percentage of Parents in Which Custody Was Not Removed Because of Kink, from NCSF

Year	Custody was not removed because of kink
2010 –	12% (13 out of 109 parents)
2011 –	23% (23 out of 101 parents)
2012 –	53% (41 out of 77 parents)
2013 –	Not available
2014 –	89% (27 out of 30 parents)

Source: Wright, S. (2015). *NCSF Incident Reporting & Response Annual Report.* Retrieved from https://ncsfreedom.org/key-programs/incident-response/incident-response.html

According to the IRR summary above, kinkier parents who come to NCSF for help have been successful in removing kink as an issue in family court and with social service workers and Child Protective Services. Of the 33 cases, 3 are still ongoing. These statistics outline significant progressive drop in child custody cases where the child was removed from the home because of parental involvement in BDSM.

These statistics reinforce the importance of professionals becoming aware and knowledgeable of BDSM as a viable culture and not ascribing psychopathology to atypical sexual practices.

Summary

Sound clinical practice is guided by rigorous applied research. Historically, research methodology has lacked critical analysis and integration of social norms and bias, resulting in biased research outcomes supporting social and cultural normative views of sexual expression and relationship dynamics. These have tended to demonize those who engage in BDSM. The following key points summarize the recent research on BDSM:

- Demographically, those who engage in BDSM represent a viable sexual minority comparable in size to the gay and lesbian community.
- There is no research that indicates clients with BDSM have a greater history of past abuse or trauma that predisposes them to this form of sexual expression. The practice of BDSM itself does not cause distress and dysfunction in individuals.

- Sociocultural and political persecutions are most likely the cause of distress and dysfunction in individuals practicing BDSM.
- Biopsychological research is reinforcing practitioners' ethnographic statements, indicating the following:
  - BDSM makes people feel good. They do it because it makes them feel good.
  - Paradoxically, BDSM increases relationship closeness.
- BDSM is a viable and healthy lifestyle.

Notes

1 http://www.dsm5.org/Documents/changes%20from%20dsm-iv-tr%20to%20 dsm-5.pdf
2 Highlights of Changes from DSM-IV-TR to DSM-5 http://www.dsm5.org/ Documents/changes%20from%20dsm-iv-tr%20to%20dsm-5.pdf
3 https://ncsfreedom.org/press/blog/item/the-dsm-5-says-kink-is-ok.html
4 Psychological Functioning and Violence Victimization and Perpetration in BDSM Practitioners from the National Coalition for Sexual Freedom. https://ncsfreedom. org/images/stories/2015_Survey_PDFs_ETC/NCSF%20Technical%20 Report%20Mental%20Health%20Survey.pdf
5 https://ncsfreedom.org/who-we-are/about-ncsf/ncsf-mission-statement.html
6 The writers of this text are aware of that the discrepancy between the total number of criminal reports (73) is not commensurate when the breakdown of the grouped incidents are tallied. When totaled, the actual number of requests for assistance with criminal issues is 72, not 73. This and other limitations support the need for continued statistical tracking and analysis.

4 Psychotherapeutic Persecution
Kinkophobia and Othering

"It is often difficult to detect when BDSM is being used in an abusive fashion, particularly if the activities involved are ones that 'squick' the therapist."
—Margie Nichols, 2005

Recent research has highlighted the negative perceptions psychotherapists have about BDSM. By having unquestioned paradigms and cultural views, psychotherapists unwittingly and unintentionally perpetuate persecution. Researchers found many instances of misconceptions, biases, unethical practices, and unwillingness of therapists to move beyond their prejudices toward BDSM and other alternative sexualities. This chapter provides a discussion and research on how therapeutic biases impact research as well as clients' experiences.

Persecution or Psychopathology

In a 2006 study, Kolmes and associates found that some mental health professionals considered kink to be unhealthy and advised their clients to give up on kinky activities in order to continue treatment. Lawrence and Love-Crowell (2008) found BDSM clients frequently report having to educate their therapists about their sexuality. In doing so, these clients may feel they are justifying their sexuality.

It is clear from the research and ethnographic reports that many who have an alternative sexuality may be reluctant to seek counseling because they fear a therapist will focus on their unconventional sexual desires rather than the client's own concerns. They may be afraid the therapist will think they are crazy or sick because of their sexual desires or lifestyle (Bezreh, et al., 2012; T. O. Brown, 2010; Holt, 2016). Many clients from the BDSM and other alternative communities have been further marginalized, alienated, and even traumatized by the unaccepting and judgmental attitudes of prior therapists who immediately tend to pathologize them (Hoff & Sprott, 2009; Kolmes et al., 2006; Nichols, 2013).

One male submissive client reported, "Seeing him was very negative. When I told him [the therapist] I was into BDSM, he nodded his head as if to say 'Ah, I know all about it!' He didn't ask what it meant for me but told me he would have to perform the psychiatric equivalent of brain surgery to cure me" (Shahbaz, 2012a).

In another case, a female sadomasochist explained, "Several years ago I sought some counseling for which I won't go into the details, but basically I was in for problem A. The therapist agreed that I had a problem with A. I trusted the therapist and thought there was rapport. Then, a few months into things, a reference to BDSM came up. So, I opened up to this therapist who, until then, had been an open-minded person. His response was almost violent. And from that point on problem A was dumped. My problem was 'clearly' SM. I needed to 'just stop.'" (Shahbaz, 2012a).

These research studies and ethnographic reports demonstrate institutionalized persecution in the form of kinkophobia by professional counselors (Nichols, 2014). This is a pattern of "othering." Edward Said first defined the term "othering" in relation to the experience of Palestinians as the demonization or pathologizing of an individual or group who is significantly different than the cultural normative and sanctioned "in-group" (Said, 1979). The DSM and rigid social norms psychologically pathologize alternative sexualities, which in turn allow kinkophobic judgments to be made by professionals with unfounded supporting evidence for these judgments. These professionals make all those who are kinky, the other, subject to bias, discrimination, stereotyping, and social and legal persecution.

Kinkophobia and Othering

In *The Ties that Bind*, Guy Baldwin first coined the term "kinkophobia" to define the prejudice toward people who practice BDSM (Baldwin & Bean, 1993). At the core of kinkophobia is a visceral feeling of revulsion or disgust; simply put, it is the outward expression of internalized BDSM negativity. It is a judgment (conscious or unconscious) about the client's morals, beliefs, values, and ethics related to their lifestyle or the manner in which they express their sexuality. It is important to emphasis that kinkophobia is most traumatic and damaging when it functions unconsciously.

For some therapists, kinkophobia may manifest through countertransference (Shahbaz, 2012a; Nichols, 2013). Transference is the unconscious redirection of feelings from one person to another, and countertransference is

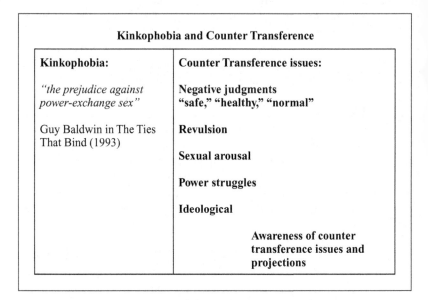

Kinkophobia and Counter Transference	
Kinkophobia:	**Counter Transference issues:**
"the prejudice against power-exchange sex"	**Negative judgments** **"safe," "healthy," "normal"**
Guy Baldwin in The Ties That Bind (1993)	**Revulsion**
	Sexual arousal
	Power struggles
	Ideological
	Awareness of counter transference issues and projections

Figure 4.1 Kinkophobia and countertransference.
Copyright: Shahbaz Chirinos 2016

the redirection of a psychotherapist's feelings toward a client or a therapist's emotional entanglement with a client. It is an unconscious internal process, difficult to bring into consciousness. It is the therapist's ethical responsibility to receive clinical consultation and, if needed, ongoing supervision to appropriately evaluate if kinkophobia or transference is impeding client-identified goals in therapy.

Many alternative sexual activities may be disturbing and uncomfortable to individuals, including therapists, whose erotic and relationship dynamics are wired very differently. Given this difference, a therapist's fears, judgments, and countertransference can strongly affect rapport in therapeutic relationships involving members of the BDSM community. Therapists are encouraged to explore how, for example, heteronormative values or feminist ideology has influenced, contributed, or created the therapist's own understanding of healthy relationships (Bezreh et al., 2012; Lawrence & Love-Crowell, 2008; Powers, 2007). Furthermore, by raising consciousness about these influencing factors, therapists are able to discern the source of kinkophobia when working with clients who are profoundly different from themselves. Without this raised consciousness about transference, therapists may become emotionally reactive when listening to some of the activities these clients may engage in. Power struggles, for example, may become a barrier, particularly when working with BDSM clients who identify as Masters, Mistresses, or Dominants.

Therapists can preemptively safeguard treatment by first identifying how, in their own relationships, they define healthy, safe, and normal dynamics. They can then develop an appreciation for the difference in how their clients define these same concepts and engage in relationships. During this process it is essential that professional counselors overtly understand conditioned negative judgments and prejudices about relationships that are different from their own, particularly with respect to defining safe, healthy, and normal dynamics.

In addition, we feel that professionals are ethically charged to correct misinformation of professional colleagues and in the general population when it pertains to alternative sexualities. To date little research exists on the experience of therapists providing counseling services to the aforementioned group.

Othering Consciousness

Developing othering consciousness first begins by critically listening to common relevant discourse, then giving a literal and metaphorical voice to topics that are silenced or avoided. Asking, for example, "How have I been othered?" enables therapists to become more conscious of their own wounding, which often gets projected onto misunderstood minority community groups and members. By identifying our own personal pain around being ostracized, we become more conscious and sensitive to others around us, and more aware of how we collude in creating and perpetuating the othering process.

By enabling those in the therapeutic community to connect with their own humanity, we can raise awareness of professional othering. From this awareness, we as psychotherapists can work to promote, educate, and understand kinkophobia as a symptom of othering. It is the authors' hope that promoting othering-awareness can transform therapeutic practices and the profession of psychotherapy, as well as research. Ultimately, understanding how psychological labeling pathologizes misunderstood minorities and can lead to persecution may contribute to healing more generally.

As psychotherapeutic professionals, it is our social and ethical responsibility to stop the cycle of misunderstanding and pathologizing this cultural group. We can do this by reinforcing the need for critical thinking and providing accurate information about emerging sexual expressions that are different from our common understanding.

Dealing with Othering Consciousness	
Othering Consciousness **Being Othered & Othering**	Understand and accept our own woundedness. Increase awareness of our own kinkophobia. Sensitize therapists to their own kinkophobia. Increase awareness of cultural social biases and discrimination in professional and academic paradigms. Question our unconscious fears of the Other.

Figure 4.2 Challenging othering consciousness in psychotherapy.
Copyright: Shahbaz Chirinos 2016

Summary

When research methodology lacks critical analysis and integration of social norms and bias, research outcomes support therapists' personal normative views of sexual expression and relationship dynamics. This bias (kinkophobia) has been codified into various professional texts, including the DSM-5, which guides legal decisions, most notably child custody cases. Practicing psychotherapists must evaluate and challenge their personal and preconceived notions by reconciling results from research that utilizes a conceptual framework that integrates an understanding that pathology and health/wellness are socially and culturally constructed.

There is bias and prejudice within the psychotherapeutic community about alternative sexualities, resulting in kinkophobia. This, in turn, relates to pathologizing clients who practice BDSM. Preliminary research, including NCSF's study of child custody cases, provides strong evidence that BDSM practitioners experience institutionalized social stigma. This underscores a lack of and need for clear clinical guidelines and best practices when working with this special population. "Recognizing situations in which BDSM is being used in an unhealthy way can take time because both client and therapist may have to counteract ingrained sex-negative feelings" (Nichols, 2005, p. 298).

The following chapter will present ways therapists can develop awareness in order to create an effective and lasting therapeutic container. It will then present client characteristics, contradictions for BDSM practice and consent, and common client issues.

5   Becoming a Kink-Aware Therapist

> *"Our role is to widen the field of discussion, not to set limits in accord with the prevailing authority."*
>
> —Edward Said, 1979

Clinical best practices with kinky clients require therapists who can acknowledge as well as understand distress and dysfunction in the context of discrimination and stigma rather than simply eliminating it by "curing" the client as a therapeutic goal (Kleinplatz & Moser, 2004). Evaluating and raising consciousness of the therapist's own bias born from normative/mainstream cultural constructs enables therapists to effectively apply the following clinical best practices toward this goal.

BDSM as a Cultural Identity

The rituals, language, and group norms mentioned earlier clearly indicate and support the notion that BDSM communities and their associated practices function within cultural paradigms. As such, clinical best practices dictate the incorporation of multicultural sensitivity and perspective in order to practice effectively (Leistner & Mark, 2016; Meeker, 2011). For this to happen, therapists need to educate themselves of these cultures' artifacts, values, and practices. In doing so, therapists can explore the client's relationship between their BDSM identity, rituals, and symbols in their specific relationship dynamics with their therapeutic goals. However, like any minority community, members will be astute at discerning and revalidate if the therapist is, in fact, open, nonjudgmental, and accepting. In order for clients to feel safe and trusted, they will subtly identify and evaluate a therapist's kinkophobia (Powers, 2007; Shahbaz, 2012a; Van Der Walt, 2014).

This chapter provides specific guidelines on how therapists can establish and maintain a culturally appropriate therapeutic container, free of kinkophobia. Common client characteristics and individual and relationship issues will also be explored.

How do therapists know if they are ready to work with this population? Therapists need to be willing to identify and evaluate their own personal bias and its sources (Pillai-Friedman et al., 2015; Powers, 2007). This openness into considering and exploring is a prerequisite for the development of awareness of personal bias infiltrating faulty clinical decisions.

Development of Awareness

Therapists working with members of the BDSM community must first raise consciousness about their own biases based on media's misinformation and historical persecutory perspectives previously mentioned (Barker et al., 2007; Glyde, 2015; Kelsey et al., 2013; Leistner & Mark, 2016; Musser, 2015). These biases impede the establishment and ongoing therapeutic alliance, which is not only needed but also is essential in working with groups who are profoundly different from the therapist.

It is important not to conflate mainstream culturally appropriate behaviors, in context of BDSM norms, with psychopathology (Lawrence & Love-Crowell, 2008; Maddux & Winstead, 2012). In order to form effective therapeutic relationships with participants of BDSM lifestyles, it is vital for therapists to deconstruct previously established and generalized notions of abuse (Connolly, 2006; Jozifkova, 2013; Kolmes et al., 2006). The authors believe that this starting point begins with the ability to distinguish healthy BDSM practices/relationships from potential psychological distress or true psychopathology.

Predominant social biases assume healthy relationships follow heteronormative monogamy rooted in a desire for equality (Barker et al., 2007; Barker & Langdridge, 2010). Therapists need to become conscious of these biases in themselves. To this end, the following set of questions are a starting point for the development of therapists' awareness on possible biases he[1] may unconsciously hold and may result in countertransference. The therapist may ask himself:

1   Do I believe relationships with multiple partners are destined to fail?
2   What were my honest initial gut feelings and thoughts about

   a   dominant men having multiple female sexual partners? How does this differ from these women not being sexually active with the dominant man?
   b   How do I feel about a submissive man?
   c   How comfortable do I feel about dominant controlling women?

3   How do my personal experiences reflect my beliefs about the expression of gender roles in my sexual, romantic, and platonic relationships?

4 How does my clinical assessment process and theoretical approach to couple and family therapy support heteronormative relationship structures verses alternative structures as defined by the client?

5 During a clinical session, does my tone, intonation, and affect change subtly when discussing traditional relationship styles as compared to other nontraditional ones in which I may lack knowledge or confidence?

6 Does my acceptance of the client require my approval of his lifestyle?

7 What aspects of the client's lifestyle I personally do not approve of?

8 What aspects of the client's lifestyle I do not professionally approve of?

Establishing a Therapeutic Container

The therapeutic relationship, oftentimes referred to as the therapeutic container, can be defined in Gestalt terms as the "dialogic relationship" and is described as follows:

> An attitude of genuinely feeling/sensing/experiencing the other person as a person (not an object or part-object), and a willingness to deeply 'hear' the other person's experience without prejudgment. Furthermore, it is the willingness to 'hear' what is not being spoken, and to 'see' what is not visible. (Hyener & Jacobs 1995, quoted in Joyce & Sills, 2001, p. 45)

Furthermore, the therapeutic container is a safe mental/emotional space, artfully created by the therapist. It is the metaphorical "place" where meaning is created from the client's expressed experience.[2]

Lawrence and Love-Crowell's (2008) basic clinical guidelines for effective therapy all fall under the heading of *cultural competence and knowledge*. Their clinical criterion applies to all alternative sexual groups, and includes both being accepting and nonjudgmental toward both the client and his

---

Cultural Competence & Knowledge

- Accepting, non judgmental attitude
- Knowledge about alternative sexual practices and values
- Refuse to pathologize alternative sexualities
- Seek supervision or consultation when countertransference issues arise
- Sensitivity to sexual minority issues
- Educate yourselves

*Adapted from Lawrence & Love-Crowell (2008)

Figure 5.1 Key elements in developing cultural competence and knowledge.
Copyright: Shahbaz Chirinos 2016

activities, as well as becoming knowledgeable about his specific alternative sexuality, practices, and values.

While it is acceptable to question and learn from a client, the client should not be the primary source of the therapist's information. Clients want to feel their sexual interests are not an issue and that they can speak with ease when they feel it is warranted (Bezreh et al., 2012; Guidroz, 2008). By probing and overly emphasizing this aspect with a client, therapists risk making the client feel objectified.

The following guidelines and recommendations can be used in establishing a professional therapeutic container when working with kinky clients:

- Validate the sociopolitical issues confronting this marginalized alternative sexuality.
- Assume that the psychological problem or diagnosis, if present, is not a function of their sexual expression.
- Affirm the client's life choices.
- Help clients with alternative sexualities clarify their needs and desires.
- Work with clients with alternative sexualities on enhancing their self-esteem.
- Help individuals get in touch with alternative sexuality communities and networks or explore their hesitation in doing so.

A desirable therapeutic container would be one that is open to non-heteronormative alternative models of relationships, is nonjudgmental, and demonstrates unconditional positive regard, which facilitates client openness and honesty and builds therapeutic rapport. Therapeutic approaches may include the following:

- Providing psycho-education and practicing insightful awareness (mindfulness)
- Reframing language and clinical conceptualization to include transpersonal psychology[3] and/or spirituality as a means to ascertain type, style, and pattern of altered states of consciousness
- Providing a clinical session to meet the client's partner(s) and affirm positive aspects of the individual(s) and/or relationship in a genuine manner when possible and feasible

As clinical professionals practicing ethically with this cultural and sexual minority group, it is important to be honest with yourself. Otherwise, the client will sense unexpressed kinkophobia, which would either hinder or derail successful maintenance of the therapeutic container. For therapists truly wanting to work with this population, it is their responsibility to educate themselves and seek consultation or supervision to further facilitate the surfacing of unconscious bias in the form of kinkophobia. The American Counselor Association 2014 Code of Ethics speaks to this issue:

- "Counselors are aware of – and avoid imposing – their own values, attitudes, beliefs, and behaviors. Counselors respect the diversity of clients, trainees and research participants and seek training in areas in which they are at risk of imposing their values onto clients, especially when the counselor's values are inconsistent with the client's goals or are discriminatory in nature" (Herlihy & Corey, 2014: Section A.4.b. Personal Values).
- "Counselors refrain from referring prospective and current clients based solely on the counselor's personally held values, attitudes, beliefs, and behaviors. Counselors respect the diversity of clients and seek training in areas in which they are at risk of imposing their values onto clients, especially when the counselor's values are inconsistent with the client's goals or are discriminatory in nature" (Herlihy & Corey, 2014: Section A.11.b. Values within Termination and Referral).
- "Multicultural counseling competency is required across all counseling specialties, counselors gain knowledge, personal awareness, sensitivity, dispositions, and skills pertinent to being a culturally competent counselor in working with a diverse client population" (Herlihy & Corey, 2014: Section C.2.a. Boundaries of Competence).

Included in this handbook are additional resources for counselors to educate themselves. The Kink-Aware Professional (KAP) list on the National

---

Healthy Therapeutic Container

Validate the socio-political issues confronting their marginalized community

Not assume their psychological problems are a function of their alternative sexuality

Affirm individual life choices

Help clarify their needs/desires

Validate & work on self esteem

Connect them with appropriate alternative sexual communities and networks

---

Figure 5.2 Characteristics of an effective therapeutic container.

Coalition for Sexual Freedom website[4] includes potential referrals one can consider when ethically appropriate. It is important for therapists to consider their own professional organization's ethical guidelines throughout the process of considering referring a current or prospective client. Throughout this consideration process, professionals are encouraged to reflect on developing "othering" consciousness and its role, as well as the political impact on members of the BDSM community. By doing so, they are also developing a sense of social responsibility.

Client Characteristics

Clients with alternative sexualities are, in many ways, very much like you, your neighbor, or others who express their sexuality and eroticism in culturally sanctioned ways (Nichols, 2005, 2013, 2014). Clients need affection, security, the feeling of being loved and accepted, and to have control over their lives.

Healthy and sustainable BDSM relationships require strong, stable, and intact personal boundaries to negotiate a sexual scene related to one's fantasies or non-normative relationship dynamics. These relationships involve considerable negotiation, which can help many people to be more introspective and thoughtful regarding what is important to them, what they want, and what they do not want.

Some clients with alternative sexualities, like clients from any other demographic, may have preexisting or coexisting mental health problems.

BDSM Client Characteristics		
Similarities between Clients with Atypical Sexualities with NON-Atypical Sexualities	• Need affection, security • Need to feel loved • Want acceptance • Want control over their lives • Have insecurities (e.g., aging)	• Have to deal with family dynamics • May have pre-existing or coexisting mental health problems
Typical client characteristics include:	**No greater history of past abuse or trauma.** **A higher level of self esteem and are healthier than average.** **Higher than average skills in communication, imagination and self awareness.** **Not necessarily caused by developmental "complexes."**	

Figure 5.3 BDSM client characteristics.
Copyright: Shahbaz Chirinos 2016

For example, they may be dealing with past physical/sexual abuse, anxiety, depression, PTSD, personality disorders, and so on. To reiterate, there is no research that indicates clients with alternative sexualities have a greater history of past abuse or trauma that predisposes them to this form of sexual expression (Silva, 2015; Wismeijer & Van Assen, 2013).

In line with recent research cited above, the authors' experience also validates those members who seek therapy generally tend to have a higher level of self-awareness, better than average communication skills, imagination, and are capable of undergoing insightful reflection.

Contraindications and Exclusionary Criteria

As a clinical best practice, therapists are charged with assessing contraindications for BDSM practice. The following table outlines some of the exclusionary criteria for BDSM practice.

Individuals who have been diagnosed with any serious and persistent mental illness (SPMI), personality disorder, active psychotic disorder, or an active substance abuse/addictive disorder that significantly or consistently impair the client's judgment should not engage in BDSM activities. It is important that therapists assess and confirm that a client has a healthy and well-developed sense of self. Clients who have one or more of the above criteria should not engage in BDSM.

Clients should not engage in intense long-term power exchange dynamics if they are lacking a stable sense of self. Again, well-established consent in BDSM practice is founded and dependent upon each individual's ongoing ability to provide fully informed consent while free of any degree of psychiatric impairment due to a transient or persistent altered mental status caused by, for example, schizophrenia and other psychotic disorders (Fulkerson, 2010; Jozifkova, 2013).

These criteria do not relate to mental health concerns such as depression, anxiety, and all forms of neurodevelopmental disorders. Depending on

Table 5.1 Contraindications for BDSM Activity (Exclusionary Criteria)

Problem	Severity
Schizophrenia and other psychotic disorders	Mild, Moderate or Severe
Poor/weak sense of self	Moderate or Severe
Neurocognitive Disorder	Moderate or Severe
Autism spectrum disorder (ASD)	Severe

Source: Chirinos, (2015)

certain circumstances, clients identified with these types of mental health issues may benefit from BDSM dynamics. Such transformative potential in the BDSM dynamic will be further discussed in Chapter 7.

Since BDSM has historically been pathologized, members have experienced social stigma, persecution, and alienation, which are most often the primary causes for members seeking therapy (Powls & Davies, 2012). From a psychotherapeutic perspective, the authors suggest using the following brief checklist to determine psychopathology:

1   Is the BDSM involvement dysfunctional to the client? How is dysfunction being defined? Whose definition is being used?
2   Is there sociopolitical discrimination and stigmatization? If so, how and to what degree does discrimination and stigmatization impact definitions of dysfunction?
3   Are the therapist's or client's perspective, paradigms, and value systems being used to make a negative judgment about the client's BDSM involvement?
4   Are all parties involved in the BDSM relationship adults? Are these adults capable and willing to provide consent?
5   Do the participants have a clear and realistic understanding of the intended (predictable) and potentially unintended (unpredictable) short- and long-term impact of the BDSM activity? Are they willing to accept the consequences of all potential outcomes of engaging in the BDSM activity or relationship?

With the exception of the first item listed above, if one or more of the items (numbers 2–5) is marked affirmatively, then consider the alternative sexuality may not necessarily be a pathological problem. Again, therapists are cautioned to discern if their personal as well as professional paradigms and value systems are biased toward this marginalized community.

According to Kleinplatz & Moser (2004), a therapist should not assume that the problem is caused by or even related to alternative sexualities. Most often, the alternative sexuality is a secondary or tertiary issue that may or may not cause these clients to seek therapy (Hoff & Sprott, 2009; Kolmes et al., 2006; Nichols, 2005). However, in some cases it can also be a central issue (Barker et al., 2007). The next section looks at some of the most common presenting issues of these clients and presents additional guidelines and practices, broadly and for specific client issues.

Common Client Issues

One common presenting individual and relationship issue may be a client or client's partner having difficulty with verbalizing their experiences and desires. A lack of clarity about this in a BDSM relationship can lead to inconsistencies, and difficulty forming and maintaining relationships. Therapeutic approaches with these clients may involve assisting them in clarifying and articulating why they are in, or would like to be in, a BDSM relationship. Exploring their personal moral, ethical, and cultural values as well as their emotional, romantic, and psychological needs are critical parts of the process that enables the development of client insight and ability to verbalize this insight (Hoff & Sprott, 2009; Powls & Davies, 2012).

Therapists may also need to assess reality testing through an informal and unstructured mental status exam (MSE). Assess client tolerance for flexibility/inflexibility and structure as well as the presence and consistency of mood congruence. Explore whether power, control, and surrender are being used as a means to mitigate various types of stress. A client's persistence in engaging with open relationships even when it stirs up extremely difficult emotions, for example, may be an indication of their lack of personal awareness between values and actions. Therapists can support and encourage a client's awareness of paradoxical contradictions and incongruent beliefs and values by reframing and meaning-making.[5]

Common relationship issues discussed below include mismatched sexualities (mixed orientation relationships[6]), difficulties arising from polyamorous-dynamic relationships, and potential disturbances to existing relationships, leading to breakups. Additional issues also include identifying and dealing with isolation, guilt, and shame, and coming out. Case studies and therapeutic approaches will be described for each issue.

Possible Common Presenting Issues	
Relationship	**Individual**
• Mixed orientation relationships	• Internalized kinkophobia
• Mismatched sexual interests or values	• Isolation
• Polydynamic relationships e.g., jealousy	• Coming out/been outed
• Infidelity	• Depression/anxiety
• Cyber relationships	• Expectations & stereotypes
• Online vs. real life	• Guilt & shame
• Long distance relationships	
• Managing transitions	

Figure 5.4 Possible common presenting issues in clients who practice BDSM.
Copyright: Shahbaz Chirinos 2016

Regardless of the client's concerns, therapists will need to ascertain their understanding of consent as it pertains to their client's BDSM interest and relationship involvement.

Discernment of Consent

As previously mentioned, BDSM and other alternative sexual and relationship dynamics seem particularly alarming due in part to the legal ramifications related to serious injury (Fulkerson, 2010; Haley, 2014; Shahbaz & Rodemaker, 2012; Surprise, 2012). The discernment of one's ability to consent is therefore of the upmost importance (Iannotti, 2014). Simply put, consent is defined as one individual providing some form of permission for something to happen or their agreement to do something.[7]

Legal definitions of consent, and the use of consent as a legal defense in cases where BDSM resulted in unintended outcomes (Haley, 2014; Khan, 2009, 2014, 2015), will not be addressed here. The focus of this reference is to present the most essential elements for therapists to gain preliminary adequacy in working effectively with representative clients in clinical settings. Refer to NCSF's website for additional information regarding legal definitions of consent in various states[8] as well as case studies. Readers are encouraged to contact the authors for consultation in addressing advanced clinical and complicated legal concerns.

There are a variety of clinical approaches for evaluating a client's ability to provide consent. Traditionally, this is completed by administering structured and semi-structured psychometric tests that include, for example, MSE. This entails the evaluation, through direct observation and unbiased clinical interpretation, of the following elements:

1 General appearance
2 Psychomotor behavior
3 Mood and affect
4 Speech
5 Cognition
6 Thought patterns
7 Levels of consciousness

It is critical to establish consent within any BDSM dynamic, whether it is a long-term Master slave relationship or a single situation or event (scene). Therapists working with clients involved in various forms of BDSM practice can verify the presence and extent to which consent has been obtained by using the following questions from the Shahbaz-Chirinos Healthy BDSM Checklist (S-CHBDSMC).

During clinical work with couples, clinicians are encouraged to explore if changes made within the relationship dynamics require the consent of all the partners regardless of the Dominant/submissive roles. As a basic rule, the writers encourage therapists to establish a foundation in the beginning that enables all parties to speak freely regardless of the client's Dominant or submissive role. The following questions from the Shahbaz-Chirinos Healthy BDSM Checklist are intended to be a guideline for therapists in clinical settings and are essential to determine the existence and degree of consent or the lack of clarity and potential of abuse of a client in a BDSM relationship.

1   *What is your understanding about consensual BDSM?*
2   *Have you discussed issues about consent with your BDSM partners?*
3   *How do you define consensual BDSM in your relationship?*
4   *How do you practice consensual BDSM?*
5   *Do changes made within the relationship dynamics require the consent of all the partners regardless of the dominant/submissive roles?*
6   *Can you choose to leave the relationship? If so, what types of support and barriers are in place for this process?*

Also consider, when determining uncoerced consent, are there appropriate contingencies in place in the event the relationship ends?

7   *Does the dominant party in a power exchange relationship demonstrate an ethical responsible approach to those under their authority?*
8   *What plans (physical, psychological, financial) are in place in the event this relationship ends?*

If a client is in a long-term relationship, it is important to explore the degree of well-being in the dynamic.

9   *Do you feel respected and valued as a result of engaging in BDSM? If so, how does this relate to your personal needs, wants and desires?*
10   *Do you feel a sense of expansion and well-being as a result of engaging in BDSM?*

Lack of overall well-being may be indicative of coerced consent and could potentially be considered unhealthy.

Difficulties in relationships may relate to a lack of clarity around boundaries established in the area of informed consent (i.e. presence of consent, changes in relationship dynamics, ending the relationship, and well-being). The questions above can be used by therapists as a starting point to assess and assist in the development of client insight regarding consent.

Relationship Issues

There are a number of unique relationship issues common with BDSM practitioners. The following section will present a brief description of these issues and recommendations on how to work effectively with these clients. This section will address mixed orientation (mismatched) and polyamorous relationships as well as infidelity (disruptions to existing relationships).[9]

Mixed-Orientation Relationships

The most common presenting issue therapists are likely to be confronted with involves mixed-orientation relationships (Barker & Langdridge, 2010). Within the BDSM, M/s, and D/s context, mixed-orientation relationships are defined as one partner who has the desire to explore or who fully identifies with an alternative sexual interest, while the other partner does not. For ease and simplicity, the former and latter will be referred to as the alternative sexuality partner (ASP) and culturally normative partner (CNP).

Partners with atypical sexual expressions or interest often recognize or acknowledge this interest later in life, well after they have established and conformed to a socially acceptable mainstream relationship (Sheff & Hammers, 2011). For many, long-suppressed or repressed sexual interests compel them to seek additional information or sexual outlets via Internet pornography. Couples may seek therapy as a result of the ASP being caught watching BDSM pornography, and the ASP and may be labeled a sex addict by the CNP[10] (Braun-Harvey & Vigorito, 2016). Another relatively common relationship issue may include a need to reconcile the desire for a polyamorous relationship (Pitagora, 2016).

Sometimes the yearning by the ASP to explore long-suppressed atypical sexual desires results in couples presenting with the need to reconcile a mismatch in their shared sexuality. These relationships may have misaligned levels of interest or complete opposition to alternative sexualities. Likewise, there may be an alignment in some alternative sexual behaviors but incompatibility in other, more broad areas of relationship interests or values.

To illustrate this, consider the following case history[11]:

John and Jane are married for 25 years and together for 30 years. They have three children, ages 16, 18, and 21. John had minimal interest and experience with fetish attire prior to getting married to Jane. He reports briefly telling his wife about his same-sex attraction and cross-dressing while dating her and prior to getting married. However, she does not recall being told or discussing his specific interests. Ten years into their marriage John and Jane progressively have less and less sexual intercourse, which coincides with him increasingly expressing a desire to incorporate fetish wear into their sexual repertoire. They initiate a trial separation, during which time they explore concurrent relationships.

Jealousy and their desire to raise their children together end this trial separation; however, it leaves John in a sexless marriage which is characterized by the ebb and flow of resentment toward Jane for requiring monogamy in a traditional marriage. John comes into therapy wanting to explore his sexual identity, cross-dressing, interest in dominance/submission, and kink. The client, John, states that his wife is unwilling to come for couple therapy because she believes he lied and withheld his interests. She also believes he needs to suppress these interests so they can have a happy family.

In sex therapy, the PLISSIT (permission, limited information, specific suggestions, intensive therapy) model is used to determine different levels of intervention for sexual dysfunctions (Annon, 1976). It is being repurposed and used as a guiding tool here for counselors and psychotherapists who are not trained in working with alternative sexualities like the case above (Taylor & Davis, 2006). It is important to note that the authors are not conflating cross-dressing and fetish dressing with sexual dysfunction.

The PLISSIT model was created by Jack Annon in 1976 and outlines the following levels, which are integrated with the above case presentation to guide readers in how to create a structure.

1   **Permission**: The therapist initially provides permission for John to feel comfortable to talk about his interests so he can explore his own levels of comfort and can voice concerns related to expressing atypical sexual interests.
2   **Limited Information**: Accurate and specific information is then provided to John about BDSM, cross-dressing, gender identity, and expression. Historical viewpoints on alternative sexualities and its psychopathologized perspectives are shared and reframed for the client.
3   **Specific Suggestions**: Therapists then provide specific suggestions and recommendations in the form of targeted homework assignments. With respect to the case above, specific suggestions and recommendations should be in line with his own values and relationship agreements with his wife. Commitment to and flexibility with monogamy and a traditional lifestyle are explored as a preface to giving homework. Exploring ethical and moral boundaries is an important part of therapy in this level. Some suggestions could include John learning about the differences between cross-dressing, transgender identities, and various labels used in various related communities. This can be done by attending social activism conferences, visiting the local GLBT center, or reading anthologies written by people with similar struggles and/or interests.

4 **Intensive Therapy**: Novice therapists are encouraged to refer John to another trained and experienced counselor if adequate clinical consultation and/or supervision is unavailable.

In a case like this, it would be helpful to meet with John's wife (the CNP). Therapists can gain a broader understanding of the relationship and the context in which this incompatibility occurs. When meeting in a conjoined or ongoing couple therapy session, the focus of treatment should be on increasing insight through a process that explores the ASP's sexual identity. This can be done by providing accurate education about gender identity formation and expression, as well as subtle and nuanced power dynamics within and outside of traditional relationships. It is equally important to assist the CNP in obtaining a referral, if necessary, to unbiased clinical support to address possible issues relating to her femininity, desirability, and to trust her ability to evaluate what is important for her. It should be emphasized that therapists providing ongoing couple therapy should strive to foster support, trust, and rapport with each client by recognizing degrees of compatibility while acknowledging differences.

Unlike the PLISSIT model, the Ex-PLISSIT model, published in 2006, involves the integration of *permission-giving* as a core feature at the beginning of each stage (Taylor & Davis, 2006). Additionally, this model requires the insightful and reflective review of all interactions with the client. By engaging in this specific process, reflection is utilized as a therapeutic tool to increase self-awareness with one's sexuality and sexual experiences by challenging assumptions.

Mismatched sexualities can also result from different values related to monogamy. People who identify as kinky and polyamorous may engage in multiple relationships with people who have varying degrees of willingness, ability, and/or competence to be in such relationships. Individuals in these relationships may present with varying degrees of mismatch and will be discussed further in the next section.

"Polydynamic" Relationships

Traditional understanding of polyamorous (poly) relationships pertains to people who participate in multiple and simultaneous romantic or sexual relationships (Klesse, 2014). There are many terms related to poly relationships: polyamory, polygamist, polyerocist, polyeros, polyfriendly, co-husband, or co-wife, to name a few (Labriola, 2010). Labriola outlined various models of open or poly relationships.[12] While all these terms describe some aspect of multiple pairings in relationships, they do not emphasize what we believe is at their core. That they are essentially dynamic and describe a relationship structure. People who practice BDSM may also be involved in or desire some form of an open relationship.

Furthermore, in the BDSM lifestyle, poly relationships exist that are not romantic or sexual. Some people in the BDSM lifestyle have chosen to refer to their multiple relationship dynamics as "family," or polyservice. These are relationships in which one Master or Dominant is in relationship with multiple submissives or slaves. Some of these pairings may cross sexual orientation: for example, a gay Master with a heterosexual female slave or a heterosexual female Master with a gay male submissive. From the authors' experience of polydynamic relationships in BDSM, many may be rooted in romantic or sexual relations; however, some are not. In particular, in multiple service relationships, in which one Master may have several slaves in service to him, deep bonds are formed that are not based on romance or sex.

In seeking to find appropriate terminology for this phenomenon, the authors sought to research various definition references. The word "poly" comes from a Greek word meaning "many," and the word "dynamic" relates to a process or system characterized by constant change, activity, or progress. The Oxford dictionary defines "polydynamic" as an adjective describing "possessing, affected by, or relating to many forces or powers; capable of acting in many ways." The authors have chosen to coin the term "polydynamic" to describe relationship dynamics that involve multiple pairings that may be, but are not necessarily, romantic or sexual.[13]

It is important to note that, like BDSM practitioners, people in polydynamic relationships have also been historically marginalized (Kaldera, 2012). This shared experience also needs to be considered in clinical practice.

Partnerships involving both BDSM including unequal authority relationships and polydynamic desires and/or practices will be referred inclusively as "poly D/s" relationships only in this specific subsection of this handbook.[14]

Jealousy and envy are significant issues related to poly D/s relationships (Deri, 2011; Parrott & Smith, 1993; Wolfe, 2003). Mismatched expectations or misunderstood agreement regarding polydynamic practice may give rise to struggles with jealousy. Jealousy is a complex emotion that is marked by insecurity, fear, concern, and anxiety. The driving force behind jealousy is the anticipation of loss of a highly valued relationship. Although different, envy is often used synonymously with jealousy. Envy is the lacking of a quality within the person experiencing envy or lacking something another person has. According to Parrot and Smith (1993), it is an emotion that "occurs when a persona lacks another's superior quality, achievement, or possession and either desires it or wishes that the other lacked it" (Rogers, 1979, quoted in Parrot & Smith, 1993). Lack is related to shame. Melanie Klein was the first to suggest that the sense of lack is associated with shame and, developmentally, shame is an earlier emotion than guilt (Kristeva, 2001).

The two broad types of relationship issues noted may result in varying degrees of psychological distress. The following case histories illustrate the nature of these issues followed by a discussion on how therapists can address them.

SASHA AND SAMANTHA

Sasha and Samantha started their relationship after meeting at a women-only event. They lived in different cities but decided to engage in a long-distance relationship. At first, they visited each other, finding their dynamic exciting. Because of their geographic separation, they decided to continue seeing others. This arrangement worked for a while until Sasha went to visit Samantha to discover Samantha was considering doing SM with another female sadist. Sasha started to make demands and set down rules, which led to conflict between them. Other women in their network exacerbated the conflict by triangulating, passing inappropriate information from one to the other. No one addressed feelings of jealousy or loss, and eventually their relationship broke down with much acrimony within their circle of friends.

PETER, A HETEROSEXUAL POLYDYNAMIC MALE DOMINANT

Peter, a male Dominant, had established a poly relationship with three women. One of these women lived with him, while the other two did not. As an experienced sadomasochist, his SM skills were admired and he was in high demand in his community. However, Peter was unable to handle the constant jealousy among the three women in his poly dynamic. There were constant hurt feelings, as well as attempts to manipulate and set one another up. Peter's lack of emotional intelligence and his poorly established boundaries allowed many personal wounds among the women. As it became clear he was more motivated by sex than the desire for healthy relationships, the women left the poly relationship one by one.

This phenomenon associated with sexual desire is reflected again in the next example.

HELEN AND JOHN

Helen and John met online then in person over a period of several months of dialogue. They thought they had found the perfect partner in the other and agreed to enter into a Master/slave dynamic. John had not had experience in being a Master, but felt confident and inspired by Helen to accept authority over her. Their dynamic evolved over time, with each enjoying the other's company and the relationship they were developing. However, two years after Helen and John started their D/s relationship, John stated he was going take on another much younger, live-in slave. Helen and John negotiated a time-limited period in which John would experiment with developing a polydynamic. John soon replaced the embedded rituals in their relationship with a more "vanilla" dynamic, dropping their Master/slave relationship, while continuing an active M/s interaction with the younger woman now in their poly dynamic. They made several attempts to understand and manage their individual needs in this polydynamic relationship. When Helen decided that she was unwilling to engage in a polydynamic, John attempted to persuade her to change her mind, but their relationship ended.

As these three case histories demonstrate, lack of clear boundaries, unrealistic expectations, long-distance relationships, and poor communication skills contribute to considerable psychological suffering. One essential goal of psychotherapy with any polydynamic relationship is to explore, understand, and affirm realistic ways in which all members can feel safe and secure as well as have a valid place within the network of consensual non-monogamous partners. Essential questions to pose from the Shahbaz-Chirinos Healthy BDSM Checklist can include the following:

1 *To what degree are you monogamous or polygamous?*
2 *To what extent are your values centered on monogamy and equality?*
3 *What are your expectations of a BDSM, kinky and poly relationship?*
4 *If this relationship is a poly situation, what is the structure?*
5 *In a kinky and poly relationship, what boundaries have been put in place to ensure each participant has a clear and respected place?*
6 *What do you do to deal with conflict or disagreements?*
7 *How have you developed your relationship skills to be in a kinky-poly relationship?*

In working with poly D/s clients, therapists are, first and foremost, ethically challenged to identify their own biases and prejudices as they pertains to individuals and couples in consensual, non-monogamous relationships (Barker & Langdridge, 2010). A therapist's ability to effectively facilitate discussions regarding jealousy and envy, for example, is directly related to their ability to perform an accurate and conscious self-evaluation of their bias in support of traditional dyadic relationships. Personal sociocultural biases need to be thoughtfully evaluated when working with poly BDSM relationships. In many instances, jealousy and envy stem from insecurities that may strongly be linked to one's fear of not being sexually or romantically desirable by one's partner, but can also be unconsciously extrapolated to others around the individual. This may lead to a sense of hopelessness for the future of other intimate partnerships. Therapists need to explore their own security with underlying core issues related to rejection, in its various forms, within their own personal relationships. To skip this process will lead to subtle and nuanced countertransference during the clinical session, and may present itself by one or more of the following:

- The therapist having an unequal focus on exploring traditional dyadic monogamy (pros and/or cons).
- The therapist's emotional (positive or negative) response is stronger toward one partner in the poly BDSM relationship. (Therapists are particularly cautioned to explore levels of comfort within themselves when a male dominant has multiple female submissives or sexual partners).
- The therapist subtly or overtly insinuates that a partner who contracted or transmitted a sexually disease into the group is 'dirty' or a sexual addict.

Cheating is defined in context of polydynamic relationships as lying, omitting, and/or withholding information directly related to the non-coerced relationship agreements and contracts, both overt and covert. Fidelity in these relationships is defined as honoring the commitments agreed on by all involved partners.

Infidelity

The Internet has been used to maintain connection between and among people in various alternative lifestyles, including BDSM. Initially, it may be a safe outlet for long-held fantasies and suppressed desires (Bargh & McKenna, 2004; Gilbert et al., 2011; Hertlein & Piercy, 2006; Lewis, 2012; Mileham, 2007; Palandri & Green, 2000). However, many have partnerships in the non-virtual world while they engage in online cyber BDSM relationships (McCabe, 2015). Some cyber relationships lead to the breakup of existing non-cyber partnerships, which may be the primary reasons for initiating couple counseling.

Not infrequently, meeting online and finding someone compatible may result in a long-distance relationship (Billedo et al., 2015; Cameron & Ross, 2007; Kelmer et al., 2013; Mileham, 2007; Rabby, 2007; Rodemaker, 2008). Struggles in navigating these issues may be brought into counseling. When people in these scenarios attempt to transition their virtual online relationships into real life, they are beset with problems associated with authenticity and unrealistic relationship expectations. Thus, grief, loss, and disappointment may be reasons for seeking therapy.

Psychotherapists are encouraged to clinically approach these cases by fostering client insight regarding the strength of and affinity to the BDSM identity and expression. The following questions related to identity from the Shahbaz-Chirinos Healthy BDSM Checklist could be used to explore these issues with clients.

1 *Why do you practice BDSM?*
2 *Why are you in a BDSM relationship?*
3 *Is the BDSM interest/relationship a core part of your identity or is it limited to sexual exploration?*
4 *Does BDSM define your identity?*
5 *Do you bracket BDSM as part of your sexual expression?*

Gaining insight into whether a client's interest in BDSM results from a sense of well-being is central to counseling process and outcomes. By doing so, the therapist is able to put client desires into context and contrast them with the non-cyber mainstream relationship. During this process, it is important the therapist is acutely aware of and monitors biased leanings toward favoring a traditional relationship. Bias may unconsciously and subtly be presented in therapy by devoting more time to or by expressing a stronger enthusiasm in exploring the positive qualities the mainstream relationship brings to the client's life. It is imperative that the client subjectively perceives the therapist as an impartial, knowledgeable and open-minded third party. The goal of any kind of therapy is to create and maintain a safe environment (container) where clients can explore their personal curiosities with insight, understanding, and safety.

If there is actual infidelity involved, the spouse who has been cheated on also needs support in recovering from the discovery of emotional and/or sexual infidelity, regardless of whether the spouse is a man or a woman. It is the contention of the authors that popular discourse and clinical training in the field of sex therapy and infidelity omit critical issues related to female spouses who have been cheated on. In these cases, keep the following points in mind:

1 Explore adult psycho-developmental issues related to sexual desirability, femininity, and body image.
2 Clarify her ability to trust her own evaluative skills related to trust with the spouse who cheated and others. (Often women have learned they cannot trust their own ability to be certain their spouse is no longer lying to them).
3 Guide the spouse in understanding the role of "fact finding." Many women want to know all the facts related to when, where, how, and with whom cheating events have occurred. Ask the spouse who has

been cheated on what she is hoping to gain from obtaining facts and evidence.

4   Explain that answers to some questions may have a negative or positive impact on her emotional state. Ask why and how would the answer help in moving her toward a particular goal.

Infidelity by a trusted partner or spouse, for many woman, trigger deeply seated insecurities regarding beauty and personal worth. This is particularly true if a sexually transmitted disease was contracted as a result of the infidelity.

Individual Issues

Some clients may come into therapy with individual issues, most notably of isolation, coming out (voluntarily or involuntarily), and feelings of shame. This section outlines effective ways of dealing with these issues.

Isolation

People may feel very alone, as if they are the only one with BDSM desires or particular fetishes. Often clients struggle with the decision to explore or act on desires they judge to be wrong, thus further isolating themselves from groups with shared interests.

By using the Shahbaz-Chirinos Healthy BDSM Checklist, therapists may explore the extent to which individuals are networked with and have a supportive BDSM community. Therapists could ask:

1   *Are they out of closet to their biological family?*
2   *Do they have friendship networks who know about their BDSM interests or relationship?*
3   *Are these networks online or in real life?*

Needless to say, clients need to receive support and resources in order to become better connected to a supportive community. Readers are encouraged to explore the references in order to assist in this process and to gain a greater understanding of the BDSM community and the individual challenges of its members. In doing so, clinicians can further evaluate and confront conscious and unconscious fears and bias that may impede the process of referring clients to potentially supportive communities and networks. Resistance to becoming or continuing a connection with these supportive social networks may include insecurities regarding not being "Dominant" or "slave" enough, and being judged by others who are more experienced and well known within these virtual or real communities.

It is also possible someone without a genuine alternative sexual leaning may be drawn into the BDSM lifestyle as way to mitigate emotional pain associated with ongoing loneliness or experiences being othered. Their "otheredness" may stem from being emotionally or physically disabled, HIV+, having a physical or sexual abuse history, ageism, or possibly an undiagnosed neurodevelopmental disorder that impedes social interactions within the larger mainstream society. Due to its acute sensitivity to being marginalized, the BDSM community has been extremely tolerant of, supportive, and welcoming to those who generally identify as alienated from society at large. (It is important to reiterate that reliable research is still needed to clearly ascertain the demographic composition of the larger BDSM community. Until this is completed and cross-referenced with other unbiased research, it is believed by the writers of this handbook that the BDSM community does not consist of a higher percentage of people with autism, abuse, etc. as compared to the larger population.)

Isolation doesn't exist only because people are kinky. People can also feel isolated and ostracized within the very same group they discover. Many marginalized groups have evolved in response to persecution and judgments, resulting in narrowly defined interests and definitions (Holt, 2016; McCabe, 2015). Some groups may establish rigid boundaries that may create inner group tensions and infighting, which leads to intolerance. Some groups narrowly define their fetishes, interests, and members (Fay et al., 2016; Holt, 2016; Surprise, 2012). An example of this is as follows:

In the northwest, there is a large diaper-fetish adult-baby community not found in other regions in the United States of America. They identify as kinky but are not BDSM oriented. If someone had a diaper fetish or identifies as an adult baby and they are BDSM oriented, they would not be characterized as part of this specific fetish community. Similarly, a person who identifies as an adult baby may trigger anxieties about pedophilia when they choose to bring their teddy bears and binkies into a public dungeon.

The authors have observed many of these groups as dynamic, often arising and dissolving membership based on personalities and connections. This creates different pressures for individuals seeking to bond with like-minded people. People may choose not to join groups because they fear becoming enmeshed in intragroup politics, thus reinforcing their isolation.

Guilt and Shame

Guilt and shame associated with non-normative lifestyle interests can also occur and be a focus of therapy (Bezreh et al., 2012; Bronheim, 1998; Nichols, 2005, 2013). Upbringing, conditioning, or societal values are contributing factors and may be based on, for example, the client's religious or cultural beliefs. Clients may feel something is inherently wrong with them, or their desires may be interpreted as indicative that they are immoral. This may cause internalized kinkophobia.

Poor self-esteem, depression, and anxiety may also be presenting therapeutic concerns. These concerns may or may not be related to a client's BDSM interests. These symptoms may be directly or indirectly caused by internalized kinkophobia, as a client may perceive themselves as being "less than" or inadequate due to their atypical interests. This feeling of being less than may be transferred to other areas of their life that do not involve sex or relationships, but are more about general security in one's own ability to make definitive decisions in one's own best interest.

Helping clients find self-acceptance to live an authentic life can be of great value and support, particularly and especially when this comes from a professional counselor who does not identify with alternative lifestyles. Acceptance precludes tolerance and approval. The profound transformative power of genuine acceptance, consistently expressed by a professional psychotherapist, cannot be overstated. By demonstrating unconditional positive regard, therapists can undo the marginalized historical context of BDSM and other alternative sexualities.

Coming Out

A therapist may be called upon to help a client come out of the BDSM closet and support him and his families during this process.

Coming out or being outed is also a significant issue. Many people fear coming out to their spouse or family. Nichols (2005) identifies that partner and family reactions may range from acceptance to horror. There are realistic fears related to job loss and unemployment, child custody, and parent guardianship that need to be explored throughout the coming out process. This is not dissimilar from what the gay community dealt with more than 30 years ago and the transgender community is experiencing currently as they become more visible in mainstream society (Klein et al., 2015). Coming out issues may arise for individuals or couples who are dealing with their "vanilla" friends, coworkers, or family of origin. Most predominantly, therapists are involved during legal proceedings such as separation and divorce.

Effective therapists acknowledge, validate, and affirm the reasons associated with the difficulty of coming out, and assist clients in determining how much to share, why, when, and to whom (Coleman, 1982). Therapists should explore with clients their purpose and realistic expectations as a result of their coming out to a specific person (Klein et al., 2015; Marrs & Staton, 2016). Once clients find a like-minded and accepting community, it often results in increased excitement in their life. This experience may be one driving force for a client feeling a sense of urgency to come out. Exploring the reasons for and impact of coming out before having the ability to succinctly

---

Coming out and/or Being outed

Fear of
    Loss of family
    Rejection by friends
    Losing social support networks

        Not recognized by
        heterosexual or homosexual
        communities.

        Results in:
            Isolation
            Alienation
            Stigmatization
            Unstable or inauthentic
            relationships

                Confusion
                    Who am I
                    What do I want
                    Is this relationship
                    a "lie"

Figure 5.5 Issues related to coming out or being outed.

verbalize answers to potential questions is crucial, as lacking this ability may alienate clients. Furthermore, it is important clients have the emotional fortitude and ego strength to set boundaries on personal questions asked by loved ones. In doing so, clients need to clarify they are most comfortable being in an educative role or simply providing disclosure.

In creating and applying a definition of healthy sexuality contextualized to the BDSM community and individual members seen in clinical practice, it is important to understand that it is first and foremost defined by the client themselves. It requires the individual to have a clear understanding of

1 himself in the context of his sexual desires and expressions,
2 how his sexual identity and expression impact himself and others, and
3 how his sexual identity and expression impair or impede fulfilling relationships.

Exploring, owning, and accepting one's sexual identity and expression are functions of this definition. These questions and considerations require clients and therapists alike to be honest and insightful in developing and utilizing introspective awareness and realization of who they are in context of their sexuality. It is encouraged that both professional therapists and clients revisit and amend this definition in order to further clarify its applicability to the client's BDSM relationships and activities. Furthermore, it can be used to assist in identifying and contrasting abuse from BDSM activities.

Notes

1 For simplicity the authors will be using masculine pronouns in lieu of 'he/she.'

2 http://www.psyartjournal.com/article/show/rosenbaum-metaphor_and_psychoanalysis_containers_m

3 Hartelius et al. (2007) provides a historical retrospective of the definition of transpersonal psychology.

4 https://ncsfreedom.org/resources/kink-aware-professionals-directory/kap-directory-homepage.html

5 From a depth psychological, meaning-making is the act of "making sense" of an experience. Another term for it is "sensemaking." It is central to transformative learning and reframing.

6 Mixed-orientation relationships are also defined as, for example, one partner being heterosexual and the other gay or bisexual. Gender identity/expression or interests in alternative sexual expressions like BDSM are other variations.

7 http://www.merriam-webster.com/dictionary/consent; http://dictionary.reference.com/browse/consent

8 https://ncsfreedom.org/key-programs/consent-counts/consent-counts/item/580-consent-and-bdsm-the-state-of-the-law.html

9 Polydynamic relationships include partnerships that do not conform to traditional dyadic coupling; the word is synonymous with polyamory. This will be described in more depth later.

10 According to an article by Voon and associates titled, "Neural Correlates of Sexual Cue Reactivity in Individuals with and without Compulsive Sexual Behaviors," major weaknesses and complications in current research involve the lack of formal diagnostic criteria. Additionally, scant sex-addiction research has led to its exclusion from DSM-5.

11 While these case studies are based on actual cases, the names and circumstances have been fictionalized to protect confidentiality.

12 Due to the breadth of this handbook, polydynamic relationships will not be explored in depth. For more information, readers are referred to Labriola, K. (2010). *Love in Abundance: A Counselor's Guide to Open Relationships*. Eugene, OR: Greenery Press.

13 Polydynamic relationships are synonymous with polyamory and polyfidelity.

14 For more information on poly D/s or M/s relationships, please refer to Kaldera, R. (2010). *Power Circuits: Polyamory in a Power Dynamic*. Hubbardston, MA: Alfred Press.

6   The "Yes But" Questions –
Controversial Psychological Issues

"It's not because things are difficult that we dare not venture. It's because we dare not venture that they are difficult."

—Seneca, 1968

People exposed to media messages about BDSM in an attempt to "liven up their sex life" may begin experimenting with an alternative sexuality without much forethought or understanding of essential concepts pertaining to, for example, psychological and physical safety. As a professional assisting in the personal growth and development of clients, it is imperative to explain the implications of their curiosity and discern the difference between healthy and potentially maladaptive BDSM behavior.

This section will explore clinical application of healthy sexuality and abuse within context. It will address specific areas of clinical consideration such as discerning the difference between abuse and sadomasochism in particular, the difference between domestic violence (intimate partner abuse) and BDSM and cutting as a psychological disorder verses cutting from a clinical, spiritual, and cultural perspective. A definition of codependency and how it can be misdiagnosed in BDSM relationships will also be discussed. Further, the nature of how BDSM relationships end and their effect on psychological well-being will also be explored. This section will further examine the importance of differentiating BDSM portrayed in pornography and actual practice. This chapter will conclude by situating the issue of social persecution and discrimination within a psychotherapeutic perspective.

Domestic Violence versus BDSM

The singular most important clinical consideration specifically related to BDSM clients involves a therapist's legal and ethical responsibility to report potential/suspected harm or danger of harm to the client or his partner(s).

This clinical decision is directly related to defining abuse within a cultural context in which BDSM lifestyles take place. In the context of the afore-mentioned historical underpinnings within the psychiatric and psychological fields, this leads to a very essential question: "How can I discern BDSM from abuse?" Leaders within the BDSM community have historically and continue to devote much time defining the difference. While recognizing nuanced or contextual differences in definition, within this text, for simplic-ity, the authors will refer to abuse, domestic violence (DV), intimate partner abuse, and the like as synonymous in definition and, therefore, will be used interchangeably.

Domestic violence is any violent or aggressive behavior within the home, typically involving abuse of an intimate partner, spouse or individual unable to care for him (e.g., a dependent elder)[1]. Domestic violence is a pattern of abusive behavior in any relationship, one that is typically intimate or sexual in nature, and is used by one partner to gain and/or maintain power and control over another. It can be physical, sexual, emotional, economical, or psychological actions or threats of actions that influence another person. Domestic violence can also involve children, either by direct abuse or witnessing the abuse of another. It is important to note variability in the oper-ational definitions of DV in historical and current research. That is, research studies define domestic violence specifically for their research purposes.

Research

Theory informs as well as creates a 'framework' that guides research meth-odology. Domestic violence research started in the 1970s (Emery, 2013) and focused almost entirely on heterosexual couples (Balsam & Szymanski, 2005; Davis, 2008; Hancock et al., 2014; Hellmuth et al., 2008). There are numerous theories attempting to explain DV across disciplines (Finley, 2013; Shannon, 2009). Some include sociological frameworks that incorporate notions of social structures as a way to gain insight into violent behaviors, whereas psychological perspectives are based on individual psychopathology as its cause. Others include family violence and feminist theories, which focus on conflict rising from family social structures and men's domination over women, respectively (Lawson, 2012). The predominant theory, patriarchal theory, justifies violence against women and children as a way to preserve domination and control (Hanmer & Itzin, 2000).

For the purpose of this guidebook other theories will not be presented. However, it is important to point out the limitations of historical theo-ries that guided research. The problem underlying traditional theories has been the assumption that DV occurs in the context of heterosexual sample groups. Until recently, research did not include GLBT and/or atypical sexual orientations and encounters (e.g., brief sexual encounters [one-night stands]). Currently, DV research does not incorporate or reflect cultural constructs related to BDSM. This lack further supports the premise that clinical research into a broader definition of DV, one that includes nontraditional (atypical) relationship dynamics, lags behind the social and cultural interests that dominate today's prolific media interests.

Consequently, when research questions are framed within this outdated context, validity and reliability are questioned: it is unclear who and what is being researched. More specifically, popularized models of conceptualizing domestic violence are gender polarizing (Bourget & Gagné, 2012), shaming men while ignoring abuse and covert manipulation perpetrated by women (Ridley & Feldman, 2003). Many of these models are ideologically driven (Dutton & Corvo, 2007; Hanmer & Itzin, 2000). Most importantly, they are inadequate because this research historically did not address people who engaged in anonymous sex, polyamorous relationships, or alternative sexual expressions like BDSM, but rather focused on male perpetrators of violence toward women in heterosexual relationships (Balsam & Szymanski, 2005; Murray & Mobley, 2009). Current research outcomes lack theories that integrate atypical sexual expression or queer theory and domestic violence in a comprehensive and cohesive framework on which to base further research (Chirinos & Shahbaz, 2015). This is the core of the problem in drawing comparisons between intimate partner violence and BDSM. Future research framed within alternative theoretical foundations focused on atypical sexualities in intimate partner abuse and domestic violence is required.

Despite this challenge, the issue at the heart of domestic violence is the need to assert power and control. What is understood from research is that a general theme of power and control underlie abuse in both heterosexual as well as homosexual relationships. Power and control are also central to BDSM practice.

In consensual BDSM authority, not power, is bestowed to another. It is based on conscious and informed consent among partners. In DV, power is taken without conscious consent or negotiation regarding limits and boundaries of control. BDSM is often conflated with abuse due to this similarity; however, BDSM is actually the embodied practice of relinquishing, transferring, or granting authority to another. The one who grants this transfer can readily take that authority away; that is, he retains power within this relationship construct. Domestic violence oftentimes involves unconscious acting out of power and control without consent.

The following table is adapted from NCSF and provides culturally contextual guidance by highlighting the key difference between an abusive and a healthy BDSM relationship.

Table 6.1 The Difference between SM and Abuse

SM	ABUSE
An SM scene is controlled.	Abuse is out-of-control.
Negotiation occurs before a scene to determine what will/ will not happen.	One person determines what will happen.
Knowledgeable consent is given by all parties.	No consent is requested or given.
The "bottom/submissive" has a safe-word that allows him/her to stop the scene at any time for physical or emotional reasons.	The person being abused cannot stop what is happening.
Everyone involved in an SM scene is concerned about the needs, desires and limits of others.	No concern is given to the needs, desires and/or limits of the abused person.
People in an SM scene ensure they are not impaired by alcohol or drugs during a scene.	Alcohol or drugs are often used before and/or after abuse.
After an SM scene, people involved feel good.	After an episode of abuse, the people involved feel bad.

Source: Chirinos, P. & Shahbaz, C. (2015). *Unspeakable Violence: BDSM & Abuse in GLBTQQI Populations*. 20th Annual LGBTQI
Note: This table was presented at the 20th Annual LGBTQI Psychotherapy Conference by Chirinos and Shahbaz.

The key elements in BDSM dynamics are those of control and informed, consensually negotiated situations in which all are concerned with each other's needs and limits. Specifically, informed consent requires all parties are fully aware of the impact of the specific type, method of play, and skill or level of ability that will take place during a scene or relationship.

Abusive relationships are out-of-control, non-consensual situations where there are no agreements or concerns to meet each other's needs or limits. The circumstances involving DV also lack meaning (ritual, community involvement, etc.) as previously mentioned in this text. Most importantly, after a consensual SM scene the people involved feel good, as indicated by a reduction in the physiological stress hormone cortisol and subjective reports of feeling an increase in relationship closeness (Sagarin et al., 2009). In comparison, an episode of abuse generates negative feelings with one or all parties involved.

Clinical Considerations

The BDSM community has worked and continues to actively work on defining and building frameworks to deal with abuse (Graham et al., 2015; Rivoli, 2015). Ethnographic reports from people within the BDSM community indicate that abuse can exist. Often these incidents are under- and unreported, particularly by kink-aware therapists, out of a desire to protect this marginalized community.[2] Discrepancies in reporting abuse by therapists is a similar phenomenon with LGBT-affirming therapists not reporting known or suspected abuse for fear of further marginalizing this community. More specifically, private, public, and government-funded service organizations are reportedly "reluctant to provide specific services to GLBT victims or they may conceal the services they do provide because they fear losing funding" (Renzetti, 1996, p. 65). Two examples of abuse in BDSM relationships are presented below. While these examples refer to heterosexual couples, similar issues have been recounted to the authors across all sexual orientations.

The first case study outlines one example of how a Master might abuse a slave, while the second demonstrates how a Dominant or Master can exploit the lack of knowledge or awareness of a submissive newcomer ("newbie") in the BDSM cultural context.[3]

Reports arose from several female slaves that a heterosexual male event organizer, considered to be a leader in the BDSM community, was abusing women. He was reportedly luring new submissive women with promises of fulfilling their fantasies. In actual practice he was reportedly engaging in non-consensual BDSM. Being new to the community, these women were not aware of the definition or role of consent in BDSM practice as the male Master withheld such education. He further commanded his new slaves not to engage with other experienced individuals within the community. Reports were initially seen as "gossip," leading to members of the BDSM community turning a blind eye for some time. Eventually, persistent and repetitive patterns of maltreatment led community members to earnestly question this Master's actions and ethical principles. Event attendees and other community members organized a boycott of his event. They confronted his actions and asked for his resignation, which then resulted in others managing his event.

Similar phenomenon to the one illustrated in the above vignette have occurred in Australia and the United Kingdom. The phenomenon illustrated in the above vignette is cross-cultural and consistent with information from interviews with various members of BDSM clubs and a number of individual interviews with slave J and slave C. These interviews also reflect the evolution of a community's ability to form social boundaries and collective rules of engagement. It demonstrates the importance BDSM community members place on complaints of abuse and their willingness to recognize and address such complaints. Many reports of abuse arise from media, magazine, and newspaper reporters co-opting BDSM practices without educating themselves about appropriate measures to protect themselves.

Many BDSM communities have evolved to encourage newcomers' attendance at basic educational sessions where they learn about the function and role of authority while retaining personal power. Currently, there is an emphasis on educating and mentoring newcomers into the community, particularly those wanting to explore submissive roles and identities. There are events that provide introductions to people who are curious about BDSM. Such organizations include Black Rose, Master/slave Conference (MsC), and South Plains Leatherfest (SPLF). Additional organizations, events, and individual mentors providing education and leadership can be found in Appendix C. Despite the enormous effort expended in informing and educating people within the BDSM community on the importance of consent, the differences between abusive behavior (i.e., DV) and BDSM abusive incidents do occur.

The next example demonstrates a different type of abuse that can occur in a BDSM relationship. The following case vignette outlines a slave abusing a Master.

> Master K and slave G had been together for a few years. Both of them enjoyed and engaged in intense consensual SM. After several years, a pattern started to emerge where slave G would show up at the homes of various BDSM practitioners complaining of being abused by Master K. They would give her shelter and reach out to Master K. When they did, it was then discovered slave G was previously diagnosed and treated for bipolar disorder and, at the time of her claims of abuse, was psychiatrically impaired. She would demand increasingly intense SM sessions from Master K. He refused out of concern for her safety and well-being. Other times he was unable to comply with her demands. She responded to his limit setting by increasing her claims of physical and emotional abuse. Friends and community members then learned Master K had been paying her medical expenses and encouraging her to seek psychiatric treatment, which she refused to do. People within their geographic BDSM community recognized that reverse abuse was taking place within their M/s dynamic and stopped being triangulated by slave G's false accusation. As a result of the community's limit setting, slave G expanded her focus to others outside of the immediate geographic area and to include people who did not know them well or their community. Eventually she had exhausted the number of people who were

unaware of her manipulative pattern. People in the community urged her to seek psychiatric treatment, which then resulted in reports of domestic violence by her Master to the police. When their investigations proved unfounded, she threatened and attempted suicide twice, precipitating her admission into an inpatient psychiatric unit for treatment.

This example illustrates the importance of understanding the ways in which various psychological disorders can easily get conflated with delusional projections of abuse as means for manipulation. The authors want to encourage psychotherapists to ask careful questions per the Shahbaz-Chirinos Healthy BDSM Checklist when taking a clinical history and, when possible, include collateral and substantiating evidence for clinically relevant claims, particularly when domestic violence is suspected. This process will require a substantial amount of time building rapport with the client and his partners.

Abuse perpetrated by one partner on another is one type of abuse and differs from self-inflicted abuse. The following section will explore non-suicidal self-injurious (NSSI) behavior in the context of seeking sensation verses abuse.

Non-Suicidal Self-Injury and Intense BDSM Sensation Play

In the film *Secretary*, the main character Lee Holloway, played by Maggie Gyllenhaal, replaces her self-inflicted cutting with a BDSM relationship. In the movie Lee Holloway cuts her body as a way to cope with intense emotional stress. A constructive Dominant submissive relationship with her boss provides a container and outlet for her need for intense sensation. This film first brought the tenuous connection between sadomasochism and self-harm into mainstream media by portraying an interest in intense sensation as originating from psychopathology. In the movie it is implied that the protagonist is psychologically unstable and/or traumatized. This misconception is rooted and continues within conventional psychotherapeutic thought without clear and supportive empirical research (Allen, 2013; Leistner & Mark, 2016).

Cutting the skin with sharp implements is one of the most alarming BDSM activities clients report to trusted psychotherapists. This section will provide a highlight of what is known and unknown about NSSI in connection to BDSM. Is self-injury pathological? The authors contend that pathology is dependent upon several interrelated factors considered within context. These factors include the specific manner in which the individual self-injures, precipitating factors, how often, and the resulting feelings the activity elicits. These factors are not isolated; assessing pathology must integrate all of these factors in a holistic manner. They should not be separate and apart from one another.

Nevertheless, the research on NSSI is not definitive because, as Stroehmer and his team conclude, "It still remains unclear whether non-suicidal self-injury (NSSI) in young adult populations represents an actual symptom leading to psychiatric illness, constitutes a disorder itself or is rather a cultural peer influence" (Stroehmer et al., 2015).

Research

Recent systematic reviews of empirical research on the phenomenon of NSSI, broadly defined and inclusive of cutting, indicate it occurs among adolescents across cultures (Muehlenkamp et al., 2012). This research predominately suggests it is most prevalent among adolescent girls and young women, and correlates significantly with other comorbidities (major depression, anxiety, posttraumatic stress, eating and substance use/abuse, schizophrenia, and personality disorders) (Briere & Gil, 1998; Claes et al., 2010; Gahr et al., 2012; Herpertz, 1995; Whitlock et al., 2006; Zlotnick et al., 1999). "Though not all individuals who engage in NSSI meet criteria for a mental disorder, NSSI is predictive of a psychiatric diagnosis" (Klonsky & Muehlenkamp, 2007, p. 124).

Research further identifies NSSI as particularly treatment resistant (Zila & Kiselica, 2001) and, therefore, subject to a high recidivism rate, which echoes self-reports from interviewees with the authors of this handbook. These interviewees, in addition, reported failure to refrain from cutting compounds their self-loathing, guilt, and shame. It is notable, from the literature, that very few employ ethnographic self-reports, with most relying largely on quantitative self-report questionnaires. While these research methods provide convenient cross-sectional data, they fail to provide detailed insight into motivations and nuances. In 2013, Gonzales and Bergstrom indicated additional limitations with literature searches:

> First, terminology differences and relative prevalence of relevant literature resulted in search difficulties. Many terms have been used to describe NSSI and most are not specific to NSSI. Some authors use these terms to describe suicide attempts or behaviors such as head banging in developmental conditions. ... the bulk of the identified articles are non-experimental or relatively low-power experimental studies. (Gonzales & Bergstrom, 2013, pp. 128–129)

Consequently, different forms of NSSI may indicate different underlying psychopathology (You et al., 2015). In comparison to self-hitting and scratching, self-cutting "indicated a higher level of distress, resulted in less subjective feelings of pain, and was more likely to be performed to relieve dysphoric affects" (You et al., 2015, p. 133). Interviews with adolescents in psychiatric institutions and in high school indicate affect regulation appears to be the primary reason for NSSI (Crouch & Wright, 2004; Klonsky, 2009; You et al., 2015).

There has been an identification of diminished pain perception among participants who engage in self-cutting (Bohus et al., 2000; Hooley et al., 2010; Russ et al., 1992; You et al., 2015). Some people have explained this diminished pain perception as emotion dysregulation (Franklin et al., 2012). Some researchers have speculated that higher levels of emotion dysregulation lead to less pain self-injurers feel (You et al., 2015) and propose self-cutting implies a higher level of emotion dysregulation (Gonzales & Bergstrom, 2013). However, these interpretations do not include alternative perspectives on pain, as is beginning to emerge in the research (Ambler et al., in press; Lee et al., 2016; Sagarin et al., 2009), which report people engaging in intense BDSM sensation experience altered states of consciousness, including euphoria and well-being. Furthermore, studies into NSSI are skewed because they predominately draw sample groups from clinical populations: those previously diagnosed with a psychiatric diagnosis (You et al., 2015). To date, there is a lack in current empirical research that clarifies the connection between NSSI, in particular self-cutting, and BDSM. In fact, the research reviewed by the authors did not include any mention of BDSM.

This lack of empirical evidence extends to treatment modalities. Few treatment interventions and protocols exist based on strong empirical research (Gonzales & Bergstrom, 2013; https://clinicaltrials.gov/ct2/show/NCT02060448). In contrast, other researchers have argued treatment protocols have not yet been extensively studied specifically for adolescents (Gonzales & Bergstrom, 2013). The writers' experience and conventional knowledge suggest that the therapeutic approach entails discouraging clients from cutting by depending on socially sanctioned coping skills or sheer willpower. With respect to treatment, Gonzales & Bergstrom (2013) state, "DBT for adolescents, developmental group therapy, and cognitive behavioral therapy (CBT) have been studied but none have an evidence base suggesting that they are any more or less helpful in the treatment of NSSI than TAU [treatment as usual as reported in clinical research]" (Gonzales & Bergstrom, 2013, p. 129).

Another typical intervention utilized by outpatient professional counselors involves referring the client to the emergency room for inpatient psychiatric treatment, the highest and most expensive level of care yet not widely available, in particular, for children and adolescents. In support of the aforementioned treatment interventions, Linehan's (2000) research indicated this level of treatment has not been reliable in providing consistent effective outcomes. Notwithstanding a higher rate of intended and unintended suicide completion, self-harm behaviors often lack suicidal intent, among other diagnostic criteria requiring admission, and insurance 'gatekeeping' (pre-certification) diverts the client back into community-based mental health treatment (Muehlenkamp, 2006), where clinicians are challenged to make sense of and provide treatment for this alarming yet not well-understood behavior.

In addition to these issues, many psychotherapists continue to misunderstand and pathologize individuals who engage in BDSM by co-opting clinical definitions of NSSI with certain BDSM activities. Consequently, those individuals avoid reaching out to therapists or receive inadequate psychological care for issues unrelated to their alternative relationship structure.

In recognition of this gap in the empirical research, Dr. Michael Aaron and his team have launched an Internet research project examining the similarities and differences between the motivations, relational experiences, childhood histories, and characteristics of individuals who engage in non-suicidal self-injurious behavior and intense BDSM sensation play.[4] Unfortunately, at the time this book is being written, results from this research are unavailable. As a result, the authors offer insights drawn from the following ethnographic field studies from interviews conducted with individuals who self-identify as using NSSI (cutting) and concurrently practice BDSM.

Ethnographic and Field Studies

While there is a dearth of empirical research on NSSI, there is a small cache of ethnographic reports into self-cutting phenomenon (You et al., 2015). However, these reports do not incorporate sample groups of people who self-cut and are involved in BDSM practice. People are beginning to talk and write about this phenomenon on social media platforms such as Fetlife[5] and online blogs.[6]

In seeking to gain some insight into this phenomenon, the authors conducted several interviews with people who cut and practice BDSM. The authors were predominantly interested in why people cut, whether the experience was different from that of being cut in a BDSM relationship, and how people who practice self-cutting with BDSM frame their experiences. This section provides insights from ethnographic accounts from people who practice cutting and engage in BDSM.

Motivations for Cutting

People who have the desire to engage in NSSI cutting behavior and concurrently practice BDSM do so for a variety of reasons. The following reasons are extrapolated from various blogs and discussion groups on Fetlife, which are specifically established for this particular group of people in the BDSM community.

There are a variety of reasons why people self-cut. These reported reasons have also been corroborated by various interviewees, of which the most common will be presented and discussed below.

Reconnecting with the Body

There appears to be two related phenomena: to reclaim the body, and to come back into the body. Both are related to dissociation from one's physical reality.

Some people have a history of physical violations, which require them to use dissociative coping mechanisms to survive traumatic experiences. Some may be survivors of rape or experienced significant and/or multiple invasive surgical or medical procedures. Self-cutting allows them to reclaim their body as outlined by the following anonymous personal communication to the authors during interviews.

> I can do what I want to my body, I hold my boundaries to others. This body is mine. (Self-report, anonymous)

In the above statement, the interviewee is reclaiming his body as his own and creating healthy boundaries for others in order to once again feel safe.

Some people report feelings of dissociation from their bodies as a result of stressors, negative memories, or experiences. These self-reports are consistent with the aforementioned research. In the authors' interviews, it is apparent that cutting enables individuals to reconnect with and 'come back into' their bodies from their dissociated states.

> In relation to the stress mechanism, it becomes an escape route from the body; an escape from the reality of the day to day. It gave me the moment to escape within myself and helped me cope with the world. I don't have that need to escape now. (Interview, slave L, March 2016)

These embodied experiences of sensation appear to center those who cut. As Raven Kaldera states, "I don't know if they were wired this way beforehand. Once they started using strong sensation as a positive tool, they needed it to keep centered in a positive safe way. The embodied experience of sensation is what centers them" (Interview, RK, March 2016). Interestingly, Kaldera also self-disclosed that he cuts himself as a conscious technique to ground and center himself in his body after constant out-of-body experiences he undertakes in his shamanic practice.

I am constantly going into altered states as a shaman. It is sometimes hard for me to come back from various trans states. I have found that sharp and sudden stimulation, like cutting provides, jolts me back into body awareness and I employ self-cutting to do so. From talking to people who are cutters, my experience seems to be similar to their descriptions about the effects of cutting. (Interview, RK, 2016)

Pain as Enjoyable Sensation

Some people report they need intense sensation; others state that the endorphin rush that results from cutting is emotionally and psychologically soothing.

I use the word 'intense sensation,' it's more than pain, it's the energy in the sensations. It has always been an amazing spiritual connection with myself, blissful. It's beyond pain. There is a ritualistic aspect which is very spiritually charged. (Interview, slave L, 2016)

The pain is there, but, within a short time it morphs into an embodied meditation. But it is not like a mental meditation, it's both out of and in the body. I am flying, free, ecstatic, but fully in the body. (Interview, slave C, 2014)

I came across an online group who called themselves 'The healthy self-masochist.' Seeing the spin on the use of words healthy with masochism gave me an insight to affirming my experiences in a positive way. I was able to affirm for myself, yes I enjoy these things, these things come from a healthy place. (Interview, slave L, 2016)

Many of the people who engage in self-cutting reflect on whether they have a neurological basis for desiring and enjoying intense sensation. They wonder whether self-acceptance early in their life for their masochism would have led to healthier self-image instead of self-loathing, guilt, and shame.

Sexually Eroticizing

Not everyone reports being eroticized by self-cutting. Those who do describe the experience of blood welling up and the sensation of opening the skin as eroticizing.

Cutting into skin is like being penetrated. (Interview, slave D, 2010)

Others describe the sensation of cutting as intensely spiritual.

The experience of parting flesh, and releasing blood is a sacred act. Blood is sacred. (Interview, slave L, March 2016)

Blood is the most primal symbolism of life. It is the life force. Being able to unleash it is powerful. To do so ritually is sacred. Yet this isn't merely spiritual, it is also erotically primal. I do experience a blood lust for the blood. (Interview, M J, 2009)

Decorative and Symbolic

Some people bring a sense of individualized aesthetic of beauty. Creating a scar is a way for some people to express a work of art, which symbolically for them represents strength and resilience.

I will be beautiful in my own way. (Self-report, anonymous, 2016)

When I see the marks on my body I feel beautiful. I watch them fade and each phase is fascinating. I want to show them off but I don't because I know others won't understand. I think they are beautiful. (Interview, slave C, 2014)

Self-marking is also a tangential quality of cutting. Kaldera reports some people he works with using shamanic methods intentionally scar as a method to remind themselves of their ability to overcome life-changing challenges and, thereby, the scars become self-empowering and self-soothing symbols of strength and resilience (Interview, RK, 2016).

Rite of Passage

Each year, during Easter in the Philippines, people voluntarily replicate the stations of the cross and embark on an ordeal path.[7] Within the Filipino community and culture, this ceremonial ritual is not framed as self-harm or pathological. Rather it is supported and affirmed, resulting in it being a socially sanctioned activity. No such cultural or social norms exist in the West.

Kaldera specifically raised the notion of modern Western society, lacking rites of passage for young people moving from puberty to adulthood, as a vacuum. He believes self-cutting may be acting as an unconscious rite of passage to fill this void. He thinks cutting fills this vacuum by providing an ordeal experience that enables people to test their limits and gain an acceptance of their own strength and capacity to cope and endure with hardship. Cutting in this way may be seen as a metaphor that fills in this gap. In traditional cultures that provide initiation (rites of passage), the entire community engage in supporting and celebrating the person's ordeal path. Cutting, as it is practiced today, is maladaptive because it is not done within a ritual container that is supported and celebrated by the community significant to the person undergoing the ordeal. The authors contend this shared experience possibly reframes cutting and creates meaning in one's identity and capacity as they transition into adulthood.

These reports require more stringent research. However, the current research suggests individuals' intentions, insight, and the context in which they cut is one critical factor in defining whether this phenomenon is healthy or destructive. Therapists can assist clients in understanding the meaning and intrapersonal outcomes of their cutting. By doing so one can assist clients in reframing cutting into a more positive path while mitigating the inherent risks associated with NSSI.

Interface with Masochism

Pain as a pleasurable sensation is not well understood, nor is its function in inducing transcendent states of consciousness or as an adjunct to healing. As previously mentioned, the conventional understanding of masochism is rooted in psychopathology based on little to no empirical reliable research and even fewer ethnographic self-reports. While it is often seen as entirely associated with sexual eroticism, this is not universally true. There are people who undergo pain as a function of obedience and service to someone they consider a higher power to themselves.[8] Others do so to induce altered states of consciousness. There are still others who crave intense sensation to ground themselves in the body.

Taboos around sexuality and BDSM make it difficult for people to claim they may have masochistic desires. Because of this taboo, these concepts and language used to convey the subjective desires for intense sensation may not be available to adolescents, let alone adults. This lack of cultural context may leave adolescents unable to articulate their experience outside of conventional pathological constructs and leave interpretations of their experience open to misunderstand and pathologizing.

> You must admit, this [the idea that the desire for pain or masochism is not pathological] is all counterintuitive. (Self-report, LGBT therapist, 2015)

Instead, when we seek out and listen to cutters who also have an interest in or practice BDSM, we find some startling anomalies from conventional psychotherapeutic thought.

Masochism has a stigma surrounding it. You must have been abused, have issues, or emotional stressors to enjoy it. Oftentimes we masochists simply enjoy the sensations of pain, the marks or scars, and/or the energy release. (Interview, slave L, March 2016)

Those interviewed either accidentally discovered BDSM or were drawn to it through latent masochistic desires. Many express relief in discovering BDSM, as it provides a framework in which they can situate, for the first time, an understanding for their craving for intense sensation. Some cutters wonder if they were born with a masochistic nature. As previously mentioned, they wonder if they would experience less shame, guilt, and stigma for intense sensation if at a younger age they had had a more positively reframed construct for their masochism.

Those who cut and identify as masochistic describe their craving for intense sensation on a continuum of frequency from occasional to a regular need/desire. Some also describe a continuum of intensity from minimal sensation, such as nail biting, at one end, to extreme sensation, like self-inflicted burning, at the other. In listening to people talking about their experiences, the idea of "good" and "bad" pain emerges.

Good pain is associated with the endorphin rush and is not associated with shaming oneself for wanting and enjoying the intense sensation. It is associated with consciously seeking out pain knowing what they are seeking and why. Bad pain is associated with compulsively inflicting pain that is not desired, not bidden, that is, ego dystonic. It is a sensation they are trying to avoid, not engage with, and they often have little to no insight regarding internal psychological and emotional drives.

For those who engage in NSSI and BDSM, the degree the person is conscious or unconscious about the reasons for his behavior is important. Levels of consciousness exist. It is the contention of the authors that exploring the degree of consciousness a person has around his cutting or his masochism is critical to discern whether his behavior is destructive. In her blog *Self-Harm and BDSM*,[9] Seani states this point well.

I think self-harm as a way of expressing emotional pain can be very effective and sweet within someone who knows what they are doing with it; but too often the self-harm is done in an unconscious and shameful way which doesn't do much to ease the person out of their state of being. Getting someone to feel joyful about their self-harm is a powerful and rare step taken by some. I generally take the view of empathy and try to frame the activity as an honest expression of true emotional depth leading through acceptance and into a place of greater understanding and possibly healing. If I was to discourage it, it would just continue but hidden from me, much like any 'shadow' practice. The only way to deal with it is to try to make it more beautiful and more sacred, more open and more normalized.... The worst thing you could do is shame the person who engages in self-harming activity as shaming is really counter-productive and drives peoples' activities deeper into the shadows. (Excerpt from blog *Self Harm and BDSM*)

Some people argue for a differentiation between masochism and NSSI. Others see BDSM as a conscious and healthy channel for their need for intense sensation. The following self-reports provide insight into how the experience of self-cutting may differ from being cut as part of engaging in an affirming BDSM relationship with another. Slave L provides an intriguing insight into this difference:

When I experience cutting from another I experience a strong con-nection, bonding, and a spiritual energy with the person involved. The energy is outward, I experience myself becoming outward, and expel-ling those sensations with another. It is like a primal dance. When I cut myself, the energy comes from my core; it's me connecting with myself. This energy is more inwards, reflective and connects me with my inner power. It is more thoughtful; it is grounding with myself and enhances my inner thoughts. When I want to think more deeply it grounds me and helps me think more deeply. (Interview, slave L, 2016)

There is a suggestion that being cut by another person can become a transformative experience for self-cutters. Raven Kaldera discussed how an experience identified as destructive and generating self-loathing from a solo perspective can be transformed into a constructive self-affirming one with the inclusion of another.

In the following example, "R" has a long history of self-cutting from a young age and has ladders of scars on her arms. She was raped as a child and became involved in BDSM in her early 20s. Her involvement in BDSM was positive, because she discovered that BDSM was a better outlet for her emotional needs, and even though she still sometimes does cut herself, she has predominantly reduced the incidents of self-cutting. She reached out to Kaldera. The following describes one of their encounters.

I remember one time doing a cutting with R. She has a ladder of hori-zontal marks on her arms. As we engaged in a ritual cutting with intent, I started ritually making more cuttings to her existing marks to transform the existing lines into runes. She would say 'I need more light' and I cut lines between the existing one to make appropriate runes reflecting her intention. In this way, we slowly turned the old scars into new embodied meaning. (Interview, RK, 2016)

This idea of another individual performing a cutting on a cutter appears to provide a container for shifting a previously negative association to a positive one. The following account suggests there is something to this idea. Slave L describes how unconditionally being witnessed while self-cutting became the turning point for her reframing her shame and guilt as a powerfully constructive experience.

The most powerful feeling I experience occurred when my master watched me cut myself. His appreciation of my connection with myself was most affirming. This experience put a different spin on my cutting, it was bonding, a spiritual exchange. I reclaimed my body. This instance discarded the negativity of my childhood. When the beauty was witnessed in what I was doing, it changed me. I felt I was being cherished and affirmed for the first time in my life. (Interview, slave L, 2016)

The function of unconditional acceptance may be a critical facet in the phenomenon of self-inflicted cutting. One of the most common self-reports from those who cut is the discovery that BDSM provides a framework and a portal to channel their needs for intense sensation through a relationship that is accepting and affirming of their desire. Most importantly, engaging in BDSM with another individual enables them to stop self-injury.

Coming into BDSM taught me a different way to think about that and take it into a different intent. I remember those feelings of escape as a child. Now I feel in charge of myself, my body, connecting with myself. The cutting and the self-play is a different place. It is more a cathartic versus an escape. (Interview, slave L, 2016)

When I'm with a kinky partner I feel no need to SI [self-injure]. I get huge endorphin and adrenaline rushes from play and that keeps me going. I can even engage in blood-play like temporary piercing and scarifications with a partner, it's safe and mentally healthy for me. It's only when I'm alone that my focus is on doing actual harm to myself, although I don't always SI when alone. (Fetlife self-report, mb)

Some people claim they would do more self-injury if they did not engage in BDSM. This suggests there is a component of needing higher intense sensation. The following excerpts from self-reports in Fetlife groups dedicated to self-cutting and BDSM reinforce this idea:

> Becoming involved in a BDSM style relationship helped me stop harming myself. (Fetlife self-report, PS)

> I'd feel less of a desperate need if I *was* involved in BDSM. (Fetlife self-report, DSC)

Clearly these self-reports indicate a more complex and nuanced perspective about the embodied experience of self-cutting, suggesting an enticing idea that cutting can be reframed from destructive to constructive when conducted within a healthy, affirming BDSM dynamic relationship. Not enough is known about how BDSM can be transformative in reframing and transforming a destructive perception and practice to constructive and self-affirming, and clearly more research is required in this direction.

The ethnographic reports of cutters describing how they differentiate their experiences as healthy or destructive, described below, speak to the process of their ability to reframe cutting.

Reframing Cutting: From Destructive to Constructive

Very few people who self-harm initially identify their experience as healthy because of the association of shame and guilt. One interview with a woman who engages in BDSM as well as self-cutting activities is illuminating. She has a history of witnessing domestic violence from the age of two. In attempting to cope with a contentious and a difficult childhood she discovered cutting. She reported her experience of cutting in her childhood:

> My self-inflicted sensations started when I was really young. I was witness to too much abuse. I use the word intense sensation, its more than pain, it's the energy in the sensations. My escape was through intense sensations. It created a reality and something outside of myself. I had counselors at the time who were ambivalent about this being constructive. My self-inflicted sensations provided a place of escape, disconnection, and I did feel a need for a lot of that in my childhood. (Interview, slave L, 2016)

The following statement from slave L illustrates an interesting perspective on how she frames cutting as healthy:

> When it is healthy the sensation of cutting comes from a place of happiness, joy, in the moment in the sensation. It is the same feeling when

someone does it to me or I do it to myself. It's emotional. It's a high, like a chemical cocktail. As a masochist I am drawn to experiencing intense sensation as a high for myself. It's a moment of time with myself and my spirituality connected to my body. Not drawn because of an addiction, not coming from a place of emotional issues. It is purely a desire to connect with myself, in a sensation that gives me peace, a knowing of myself. (Interview, slave L, 2016)

The idea of shifting the stigmatized, negative frame about cutting to a more positive or healthier one is reinforced by others. Raven Kaldera is an author and educator on alternative sexuality and spirituality. He is trained as an ordeal master, using a variety of techniques, including cutting and branding.

I recognized that for those doing self-harm from a place of self-loathing was not a good reason. I started to explore ways of enabling a shift of perspective in which cutting could come from a place of self-acceptance, strength and security by asking "as an ordeal master, what can we do to make this a positive process for you." Over time, I came to recognize the process of requesting it was an important element of moving from trusting self to trusting another to do cutting. Similarly, doing it for a special purpose/intent in a ritualistic context with proper hygiene, proper instruments, and proper skills enables turning the phenomenon from a shameful negative into a positive. Subsequently, many self-cutters seek me out wanting me to use my skills in a ritual setting to help them evolve. (Interview, RK, 2016)

Another interesting phenomenon relates to the issue of marks left from cutting, scarification, and other forms of intense BDSM activity. As described above, the context within which scars are formed informs whether or not a positive or negative association becomes created.

The marks embody reality. I can touch them, become mesmerized by them. When I cut from a place of escapism, I felt shame. Now when I mark myself or am marked by another, these marks morphed into appreciation. (Interview, slave L, 2016)

The marks help me cope. I like to look at them, touch them, trace them. When I do, it centers me, calms me, makes me feel blissful. (Interview, C, 2014)

Another cutting I did involved using ash rubbed into the cutting to bring about a scarification as part of a ritual for growth and truth. I cut a spiral of two inches tall that wound in and out. The scars I made keloid as intended. The new scars serve as a coping mechanism for her to this day. When she is upset and/or losing touch, she will trace the scar to center herself. It really helps her. (Interview, RK, 2016)

Self-inflicted marks and those imposed on me have distinct differences in level and intent. The self-inflicted marks will fade quickly. I don't wish them to be more powerful than my marks from my Master. My master enjoys creating differences in their marks. His marks are imposed on me, not in my control therefore they have a different meaning to do with his authority over me. The self-inflicted marks are private, they have inner connectedness. (Interview, slave L, 2016)

Such accounts suggest reframing cutting could be constructive and even therapeutic. Further ethnographic research into this phenomenon is required to understand this multidimensionality and complexity of NSSI cutting performed in a BDSM context.

Call for Future Research

These ethnographic field reports clearly indicate that intent and context are very important in determining whether one engages in NSSI is in danger of true suicidality or seeking intense sensation. Lacking substantiating research, the authors contend the degree of consciousness and reflection individuals bring to bear on these activities, and the context within which they occur, form the basis of a positive or negative metaphorical (psychological) container.

Pain and suffering have been pathologized in Western civilization and augmented through psychological theories that have been manifested through research and practices. The willingness to explore feelings associated with pain and suffering have, across times and cultures, held a valuable place in the development of character and been a source of transformation through self-reflection. The clinical intervention of self-reflection, in this process, has functioned as a sacred and spiritual path to enlightenment.

There is a transpersonal quality associated with these insights. Mainstream psychological and clinical best practices are devoid of transpersonal concepts and "other ways of knowing." Subsequently, psychological thought into novel phenomena with scant or entirely lacking research fails to take these qualities into account in developing alternative frameworks of understanding. Detached from the meaning-making inherent in cutting and BDSM, the tendency to pathologize these activities and individuals continues. At the heart of this reaction is the client's fear of being judged. This fear of judgment leads to the avoidance of seeking clinical help.

The challenge for researchers and therapists lies in questioning existing formal and informal paradigms that inform judgment as well as exploring alternative interpretative frameworks in seeking to understand the phenomenon of self-cutting in and outside the context of BDSM: in particular, not pathologizing pain and suffering, and enabling clients to explore and accept the purpose and meaning in these drives without misinformed judgment.

For example, psychotherapists can utilize a non-literal and metaphorical approach typical of transpersonal and analytical psychology to interpret the client's inner and outer worldview. Exploring and clinically applying these interpretations to their therapeutic goals and challenges could lead to insightful information, clarification, and development of belief structures, intra- and interpersonal awareness, as well as situating their social and emotional experiences within a broader meaning-making context.

Future research is desperately needed in this area, in particular, to further clarify and determine intense sensation-seeking versus true suicidality. The authors look forward to the results from Dr. Michael Aaron's research in shedding further light on NSSI behavior and intense BDSM sensation play. More research is needed to explore ways in which psychotherapy can create an affirming container for people who seek to experience intense sensation.

The authors believe psychotherapy needs to re-envision and re-mythologize the role of pain as valuable rather than pathological. Without such a shift in the psychotherapeutic community, a constructive theory will be difficult to create and, therefore, impede much-needed research into this phenomenon. Future research needs to explore this phenomenon from a nonjudgmental and broader perspective for understanding the constructive role of pain and suffering.

Codependency in BDSM Relationships

One of the hallmarks of abusive, as well as addictive, relationships is the presence of codependency. Since its inception in the 1980s there have been many definitions attempting to provide a foundation for understanding. Gierymski & Williams (1986) proposed a medical (disease) model, citing it as a diagnosable yet treatable disease with specific physical symptoms while originating from childhood familial patterns. O'Gorman and Oliver-Diaz further clarify it as

> a form of "learned helplessness" and comprises a learned behavior system consisting of family traditions and rituals taught from one generation to the next concerning how the family teaching intimacy and bonding. (O'Gorman & Oliver-Diaz, 1987, in O'Gorman, 1993, p. 203)

In 1990 it was further added, "When codependency is viewed within this context it comprises a type of relationship disorder" (O'Gorman, 1990). Melody Beattie (2013) defines codependency as "one who has let another person's behavior affect him or her, and who is obsessed with controlling that person's behavior" (Beattie, 2013, p. 34).

The definition of codependency continues to evolve in the DSM. Cultural and sociological research refutes codependency as a useful diagnostic category, as it disempowers the individual (O'Gorman, 1993). Sociocultural contexts are important in defining codependency as a pathological disease. This has significant bearing in the use of codependency as a label when addressing authority-imbalanced relationships occurring in BDSM.

Determining codependency in BDSM relationships requires therapists to use a cultural perspective while integrating an understanding of power dynamics. Various critics have refuted the clinical conceptualization and futility of codependency, citing unequal sociopolitical power distributions within relationships where traditional gender roles are accepted. They argue that models of codependency, in part, are inadequate because they do not account for "unequal distribution of power and resources, the lack of options, the blatant sexism, racism, homophobia and violence encountered toward women" (Brown, 1990, cited in Anderson, 1994, p. 679). Various authors further contend that models of codependency do not address relationships comprised of individuals who *consciously* engage in unequal power dynamics, for example, BDSM (Brown, 1990; Humes, 1989; Krestan & Bepko, 1990; Walters, 1990; Wetzel, 1991). The authors recognize this gap in research. Their suggestions have been modified and integrated with the authors' insights for the purpose of offering readers the following clinical guidelines for practice.

During some BDSM scenes and in M/s relationships, one partner does control the other through a conscious exchange of authority and, most likely, one or both parties depend on the other for fulfillment in some way. These are intentionally consensual, non-equal authority dynamics that contradict socially ascribed models of healthy egalitarian relationships. Their atypical power structure should not automatically be conflated with codependence. The therapeutic challenge for therapists working with members of the BDSM, and, in particular, M/s community lies in discerning this difference.

If consensual unequal authority dynamic relationships are done correctly, there is a continuous and concerted effort in being conscious of this unequal authority distribution as well as how and when it plays out. The most important difference is that unhealthy codependence and enmeshment are unconscious, unintentional, and are ascribed to an ego-dystonic psychological phenomenon.

Modern Western society is driven by unquestioned values related to equality, individualism, and heteronormative monogamy. These characteristics are cultural influencing factors that pervaded Western psychological thinking. Oftentimes, these cultural constructs are construed as normal and applied to all relationships.

Therapists need to question this thinking by questioning their own social and cultural paradigms while being very careful not to apply traditional codependent labels to alternative relationships. Additionally, therapists need to be sensitive to the BDSM-specific cultural values and artifacts. As the research indicates, those drawn to express their submissive needs in BDSM relationships are not necessarily lacking self-esteem. In fact, many hold responsible roles and jobs and are capable of self-sufficiency. Their choice to serve and obey another is conscious and consensual, while understanding that their personal power is not relinquished along with their personal authority. As previously mentioned, power is retained regardless of the role one embodies within the relationship.

There is a growing interest in BDSM and power-exchange relationships ranging from Matt Haber's article "A Hush-Hush Topic No More"[10] in the *New York Times* to dissertations and articles (Barker, 2013; Benz & Benz, 2015; Leistner & Mark, 2016; Magliano, 2015; Martin et al., 2011; Musser, 2015; Rodemaker, 2008) to hotels cashing in on the Fifty Shades theme,[11] as well as numerous online how-to advice.[12] Some people may be drawn to these dynamics predominantly from two forms of unhealthy positions. First, for those who do not have a clear core sense of themselves and need someone else to take care of them, the draw to these relationships originates from an unhealthy motivation.[13] Second, those who are overcompensating for a personal lack may be drawn to control and dominate (Masters, 2009; Rinella & Bean, 1994; Warren, 1998). In this case their dominance is compensatory as opposed to a reflection of an insightful awareness and expression of their true personal identity and core desires.

In either situation, therapists are advised to identify whether previously existing psychological problems currently exist. Clinical assessments, including theoretical frameworks for abnormal psychology, must incorporate culturally sensitive constructs specific to alternative sexualities, including BDSM. A thorough therapeutic history would determine the degree of consciousness around issues of a client's subjective feelings of lack as well as interest and motivation to become involved in a BDSM relationship. Does the client have a history of difficulty identifying his own feelings, making self-affirming decisions, lack of self-trust, or other self-limiting thoughts, feelings, and behaviors? Is he exhibiting overcompensation in other areas of his life? Does he have clearly a defined purpose, vision, or philosophy about his BDSM practice? Is he seeking a BDSM relationship as a way to escape feelings of inadequacy? Is a Dominant or Master seen as a rescuer to avoid doing what the client does not want or does not feel capable of doing? Are the client's values and behaviors aligned? These questions are reflected in the Shahbaz-Chirinos Healthy BDSM Checklist.

If the responses to these culturally sensitive questions indicate a lack of clarity, low self-esteem, or overcompensation, the therapeutic direction needs to consider counseling these individuals not to engage in extreme BDSM relationships or activities until they have a stronger sense of self.

Ending a BDSM Relationship

There are many different ways one can end a D/s or M/s relationship. This is known as "uncollaring" or "releasing" from service. A submissive partner can request to leave a BDSM relationship, or they can be abandoned. The impact of being released or abandoned can leave a resounding negative imprint on both the submissive as well as the Dominant partner.

BDSM relationships end for numerous reasons, including divorce and death. In power-exchange relationships, submissive partners may seek to be uncollared to pursue other interests such as a new job or another relationship. Ultimately, the reasons for uncollaring are numerous and may include admission into inpatient psychiatric treatment, incarceration, or irreconcilable differences. Often, like most relationship failures, they may be abrupt, unwanted, and not mutual. However, unlike traditional relationships, if there is a strong unequal authority dynamic, it can make these endings profoundly vulnerable to extreme psychological distress, leading up to and including suicide. When uncollaring occurs, it has a profound psychological impact on all members of the relationship, and its impact is correlated with the depth of their practice. The structure that was once in place is now broken.

Clinicians working with members in alternative lifestyles may have clients who come into therapy seeking support in understanding issues related to abandonment, loss of structure, or loss of self or identity. The termination of a long-term BDSM relationship adds complications that therapists need to be aware of. The following case examples illustrate this importance.

> Example 1: I had been in an eight-year, long-distance Master/slave relationship. Master and I would meet at conferences. Everything in my daily routine was according to his protocol. When I rose, what I ate, what I wore. He controlled my sexuality. I was only allowed to orgasm when and how he wanted me to. After he attended Landmark, he decided he had to honor his vows to his marriage, and he could no longer be with me. He was married to a woman who was not into BDSM. He released me over the phone and without any preparation or

forethought. I was devastated. One day my life had structure, meaning and purpose; the next, nothing. At the time, I did not know other people in the Master/slave lifestyle. I knew kinky folks, but no one could understand the depth or meaning of the dynamic I had lost. I became suicidal and nearly went through with a well-thought-out plan devised to end my life. I was unable to have an orgasm for nearly three years after. Every time I touched myself, I was filled with grief and loss. These were the darkest days of my life. I realized that despite being released, I am and will always be a slave. It is the core of my being. I also learned the importance of connecting with others like me. (slave K, 2010)

Example 2: After Master K died, I lost it. I was the one who had to agree to honor his "do not resuscitate wishes" in the hospital. I was the one who made the funeral arrangements and memorials – one for his biological family, one for his leather family. He left me a sizable inheritance. After he died I lost it, I relapsed. When we had met back in 2005, as part of his conditions and his rules, I had to stop doing heroin. I had been clean and sober for over 7 years. With him gone, there was no more meaning in staying sober. All the friends and community we had built around us flocked around me for a short while, then disappeared. Without any structure, I spiraled back into using drugs again. I had the money, the means and the contacts were easy to find. I went through my inheritance like it was water, until I was homeless. All my self-loathing, my desperation, and loneliness found respite in being high. People, in general, including friends within the community moved away, intentionally, or unintentionally. I know now I pushed them away. (slave R, 2011)

Involvement in consensual unequal power dynamic relationships provides a profound sense of security. This sense of security and other feelings are embodied as a result of the rituals and protocols embedded in the nature of BDSM relationship dynamics. An unplanned and/or abrupt termination of this highly secure and intimately bound relationship may lead some individuals to contemplate or pursue suicide as a means to end their psychic pain.[14] It is noteworthy to state that this, more than likely, will not be the initial or primary reason for therapy. Thus it is import for clinicians to be mindful of related issues.

Regaining autonomy and personal agency after the end of a relationship requires time and professional as well as social support. This experience may be akin to a divorce, with people in the couple's social circle likely to take sides. As most of these relationships are marginalized, the available social support structures may disintegrate. Individuals may choose to leave the

BDSM community, becoming increasingly isolated in respect to the number of people who may genuinely empathize or support them. Some who choose to stay may begin to withdraw from the individual who leaves as a way to protect themselves and the community from further "othering" or demonization.

Sometimes support is not possible from within the BDSM community. A failure in BDSM relationships raises uncomfortable unconscious fears within the community (Graham et al., 2015). Community responses to people who choose to end their relationship may vary: shunning, or spreading disparaging rumors about one or all of the members in the relationship, can ensue.

However, from ethnographic reports and interviews of people in the BDSM community, there appear to be conscious and supportive ways to end BDSM relationships. An example of this is the use of ritual.

> When my Master decided it would be in my best interest to be released, I was sad, but, agreed. We had reached the end of our journey together. I recognized what he was doing was painful for him as well, but that he thought it best in the long run for me to find someone else. He decided to uncollar me in a ceremony to which he invited the other members of our leather family. I shall never forget the day that happened. We all assembled in his dungeon. He invited each member of the family to make a statement if they wished. I had bought him a small gift, which I proceeded to give him along with a poem from Rumi. He had tears well up in his eyes. It was very moving saying good bye to him. He took the collar off, broke the lock and gave it to me to keep. It was then his turn to say something. He told us he had been inspired to do a blood ritual. He took his leather shirt off, laid it neatly on the chair, then taking a scalpel, he did a cutting over his heart. When I realized what he was doing I dropped to my knees, overwhelmed with love. He was symbolically cutting open his heart. He made an imprint of his blood on a white handkerchief and gifted it to me as a symbol of his loving sacrifice. The rest of the family was flabbergasted. He explained, that just because our Master/slave dynamic had ended, it didn't mean the love we had for each other would end, but rather, would go on in perpetuity. He told everyone I was always going to be part of his family. The unconditional love between us was palpable then, and continues till this day. He and I will always be deeply connected at a primal level. (slave C, 2009)

As these relationships are highly ritualized, particularly when people enter into them, the use of an ending ritual has great benefit, particularly when conducted within the community. These rituals provide the individuals concerned with respect and completion, and provide the community a sense of clarity around what is being asked of them after the ending of the relationship.

Sources of support and appropriate resources for those who choose to leave the lifestyle/community can include referring to elders in the community, who can provide a network of support.

Therapists need to evaluate the client's harm to self in particular, as well as risk of suicide attempt, help-seeking behaviors (historically and currently), and access to formal (professional) and informal (community) support. The authors recommend connecting isolated individuals with the BDSM community. It is advisable that therapists seek out additional support and consultation in the event individuals are resistant to getting community support.

BDSM Pornography versus Reality

As this marginalized community gains prominence and recognition through social media and Internet pornography in particular, people have been drawn to explore long-suppressed, cherished sexual urges or fantasies (McKee, 2005). For many, these urges are not identified or associated by the client as having a link to BDSM practice. While the Internet has become an engine of connection, it has also been responsible for the propagation of misinformation by inaccurate portrayals in pornography (Achola, 2014; Rambukkana, 2007; Schussler, 2013).

BDSM pornography invariable portrays heterosexuals in SM acts, which are typically unsafe and non-consensual. The person who is cast in the role of the Dominant or top is often portrayed as an irrational destructive boor, punishing ridiculous transgressions at a whim. In particular, female dominants are portrayed as stereotypical caricatures of power-hungry, uncaring women. The bottoms are often depicted as being ensnared against their will, non-consensually. Worse still, the 'slave' is often depicted as acting out in a brattish manner to be 'punished.' Often, sadomasochist acts are brutally depicted with little emphasis on safety or skill development. These pornographic images do not reflect the real-life practice of BDSM or its culture (Prior, 2015). Furthermore, pornography is not in any way capable of conveying the energetic dynamic between submissive and Dominant during a scene. Unfortunately, these images are assumed to be the "norm" by curious newcomers lacking knowledge of the sociocultural and emotional context in which these practices occur.

As a result of the boom of online connectivity, the tightly knit culture of BDSM communities are in danger of becoming diluted – of losing the roots and cultural context from which they have originated in modern history. The Internet has provided ready access to sexual predators who troll online for newcomers, promising to fulfill long-held fantasies, only to deliver abuse. Dabbling in BDSM can be dangerous if one is not aware of these pitfalls.

People in real-life BDSM culture generally advise those wishing to explore this alternative sexuality to take steps to remain safe. It is advisable to DO the following things:

- **Know yourself.** Why are you interested in BDSM? What is your motivation? Is this a sense of being (identity) versus a fad that you want to explore?
- **Educate yourself.** Go to BDSM events, meetings,[15] and BDSM conferences. (There are numerous workshops and conferences devoted to learning particularly for interested people. Going to these enables newcomers to understand the risks involved as well as to learn real-life BDSM practices.)
- **Don't rush into relationships.** Take your time to explore and understand your play partner. BDSM relationships are like any other relationship: you need to have more than sexual compatibility to have a sustainable relationship. At the very least newcomers need to be aware of their and their play partner's medical health, STDs, and relationship status. These relationships often start online. As such, it is wise to ask for the person's real name and contact information as well as have others know whom the newcomer is meeting with and where.
- **Know who you are with.** Ask details about their experience and their level of skill in BDSM in general, and with specific activities. It is important to know whether a person has spent time acquiring skills in the type of fetish or practice/play in which they proclaim to be an expert. There are numerous workshops in every state and across the nation teaching BDSM skills. The person online should be able to name one or two individuals or events at which they developed these skills. This allows the newcomer to know if the person is genuine, known, and displays appropriate BDSM values.
  - This also goes to understanding how different scenes impact attachment and its link to your play partner.
- **Get real-life references.** Ask the person you are playing with for community references who would vouch for them. If the person is legitimate and bona fide, they would be known in the BDSM community and would have no problem providing references to vouch for them. Again, this demonstrates that they understand and conform to real-life BDSM culture.

The BDSM community advises people to **NOT DO** the following things:

- Do not enter into an SM experience or relationship with the first person you meet online who promises to fulfill all your fantasies.

- Do not engage in BDSM without understanding the stages of a scene (negotiation, play, and aftercare) and how they are specific to you and your play partner.
- Do not engage in any activities while using drugs and/or alcohol.
- Do not engage in a BDSM scene without having a basic understanding of your experience, interests, and limitations.
- Do not lose focus of your limitations during a scene or your motivations for having a scene with a particular Dominant or submissive.
- Do not engage in a scene or relationship without being clear of your internal and external motivating factors.

In Summary

The topics raised in this chapter are controversial and contentious but important to bring to awareness. They reflect on and highlight biases and weaknesses in the research in these areas as well as in current psychotherapeutic practices.

There is a clear need for therapists to understand how social media sensationalizes BDSM activities. By having clear personal and clinical perspectives one is able to discern sensational controversy from reality and mitigate exceptional issues in therapy. Once this is successfully done one is able to consider various transformative aspects of BDSM practice.

Future research rooted in ethnographic reports from practitioners is required to understand and clarify the difference between consensual BDSM and domestic violence, the role of BDSM in transforming destructive and self-loathing aspects associated with NSSI, distinguishing codependency from consciously chosen relationships engaging in unequal authority exchange, and in understanding the role of pornography in the evolution of and expression of sexuality.

Notes

1 It is important to note that incidents of intimate partner abuse can occur within a broadly defined relationship where the partners are not cohabitating. It can also include sibling bullying within the home.

2 The authors contend that failure to report is a failure to exercise social responsibility to the community in which he practices as well as the larger community. For additional information readers are encouraged to contact the American Psychological Association, Psychologists for Social Responsibility.

3 Term applied to people who are new to the BDSM community and express a desire to engage in, learn about, and explore their BDSM desires.

4 Call for participants in survey examining "Differences between BDSM Participants and Individuals Who Engage in Non-Suicidal Self-Injury"; https://uwstout.qualtrics.com/SE/?SID=SV_5q1GgTf9bUHeGy1

5 Fetlife is a free social media platform dedicated to people across all sexual orientations who engage in or want to explore BDSM, or kinky or fetish interests. It is predominantly a site for communication and commentary, where members can post and discuss issues that matter to them. It is not a dating site.

6 http://www.crazyboards.org/forums/index.php?/topic/35113-kink-vs-self-injury-is-there-crossover/

7 For more information on this phenomenon, see Laura Wagner's report on NPR in 2016, "Filipino Devotee Crucified in Annual Ritual – For The 30th Time"; http://www.npr.org/sections/thetwo-way/2016/03/25/471888602/filipino-devotee-crucified-in-annual-ritual-for-the-30th-time, and Richard Grennan's 2012 documentary *The 26th Crucifixion of Ruben Enaje*. https://www.youtube.com/watch?v=zNpNR7uYgFQ as well as "Filipino fanatics re-enact crucifixion for Good Friday." which aired on the Australian Broadcasting Corporation in 2012 http://www.abc.net.au/news/2012-04-06/philippino-fanatics-crucify-themselves-for-good-friday/3937448

8 Those who practice nonsexual masochism are labeled as "service masochists" within the BDSM community.

9 http://www.seanilove.com/self-harm-and-bdsm/

10 See Matt Haber, Feb. 27, 2013. "A Hush-Hush Topic No More"; http://www.nytimes.com/2013/02/28/fashion/bondage-domination-and-kink-sex-communities-step-into-view.html

11 Fifty Shades of Grey–style hotel planned in Grade II listed Kent building; http://www.mirror.co.uk/news/weird-news/fifty-shades-grey-style-hotel-7545267

12 http://www.refinery29.com/bondage-sex-play-bdsm;
http://narrative.ly/the-dominatrix-class-that-changed-my-life/
http://mic.com/articles/121288/bdsm-experts-fact-check-the-new-50-shades-book-and-the-results-aren-t-good#.8bdK0TqGx
http://www.huffingtonpost.com/sandra-lamorgese-phd/edge-play_b_9473490.html; http://www.huffingtonpost.com/sandra-lamorgese-phd/turn-bedroom-into-red-room_b_8691676.html
http://www.psmag.com/books-and-culture/bondage-sm-aficionados-better-adjusted-than-most-58723
http://www.huffingtonpost.com/ja-rock/bdsm-and-mental-health_b_9227222.html

13 http://www.paganbdsm.org/brokentoys/

14 Go to http://www.sprc.org/sites/sprc.org/files/library/srisk.pdf for additional information regarding risk and protective factors associated with suicide.

15 Some meetings are often known as "munches" or lunch meetings, where people socialize and meet one another with no BDSM activity.

7 Into the Psychotherapeutic Borderland

"The only true voyage of discovery ... would be not to visit strange lands but to possess other eyes, to behold the universe through the eyes of another, of a hundred others, to behold the hundred universes that each of them beholds, that each of them is."

—Marcel Proust, 1929

In this section, the physical and psycho-spiritual transformative aspects and qualities of BDSM practices and relationships will be discussed. The three transformative aspects of BDSM include (1) qualities inherent in pain and suffering, (2) characteristics in BDSM relationships, and (3) characteristics of BDSM community. Utilizing the authors' ethnographic research through interviews of participants as well as workshops conducted by members of the BDSM community, participants' views of the transformative practices in community, relationship, and pain experience will be explored.

Sacrifice and suffering are essential aspects of many psychosocial transformative methods within tribal communities around the world (previously discussed in Chapter 2). In the modern Western world, physical transformative aspects of BDSM are beginning to be identified through psychobiological research (Ambler et al., in press; Lee et al., 2016; Sagarin et al., 2015). This research further corroborates the author's research finding from numerous interviews with BDSM participants. As described earlier, this groundbreaking research is providing biopsychological explanations for the transformative elements of pain and suffering. Fundamentally, the physical and emotional/spiritual aspects of control/surrender inherent in BDSM practices are capable of creating transformative experiences through a process of dissolving the ego, although these experiences are not well understood within a psychological paradigm (Lee et al., 2016; Sagarin et al., 2015).

Psychological paradigms have increasingly adopted a reductionist empirical scientific perspective and discourse, which ignore embodied and energetic phenomenon (Hartelius et al., 2007; Hillman, 1975; Lukoff, 2012). Additionally, the medicalization and commercialization of Western psychology has increasingly pathologized suffering in service to a culture that values "quick fixes," even for complex problems. By framing suffering as a "problem" needing fixing, psychotherapy itself is losing connection and knowledge of the psycho-spiritual transformative benefits of suffering, sacrifice, and ordeal work (Hillman & Ventura, 1992; Weiss, 2006). As such, popular modern psychological language and discourse do not have the theoretical framework or language to structure and facilitate meaningful discussions about the transformative nature of BDSM experiences. Mainstream psychotherapists are encouraged to look outside[1] of limited psychotherapeutic paradigms for instructive alternative frameworks in which obedience and services as well as the ordeal path are seen as sacred transformative paths (Glucklich, 2001; Grof, 2008; Kaldera, 2006).

Mainstream evidenced-based psychotherapeutic approaches do not have the appropriate or adequate theoretical constructs with which to develop an understanding of the aforementioned phenomenon. Recently, scholars frustrated with the inability of mainstream psychology to explain various phenomena that transcend the personal have looked into bridging fields. Depth psychological constructs such as transpersonal psychology and the study of somatic embodiment (Allen, 2013; Hammers, 2014; Knight, 2014; Ramsour, 2002) provide theoretical frameworks and models that more readily enable an understanding of the transformative experiences of BDSM.[2] Transpersonal psychology is defined as an integration of humanistic psychology and spirituality, which also includes honoring altered states of experiences (Glucklich, 2001; Grof, 1985, 2008; Moss, 1999). Thus, it encompasses how meditational, mystic, and psychedelic experiences contribute to awareness and sensemaking of suffering and complex problems. Essentially, embodied experiences are a means of meaning-making that are separate and apart from cognitive understanding. In other words, the embodied experiences BDSM practitioners report are grounded in and are facilitated by non-cognitive processes that lead to meaning-making. The bias[3] in Western science, which has filtered into the field of psychology, essentially continues to ignore and dismiss dialogue about these constructs.

Another useful perspective comes from depth psychological approaches, which explore the subtle, hidden, and marginalized as well as unconscious aspects of human experience. A *depth* approach may include therapeutic traditions that explore the unconscious, and involves the study and exploration of metaphors, myths, complexes, and archetypes. A particularly useful construct that has been used by practitioners in the BDSM community for personal development purposes is the notion of the "shadow."

The "shadow"[4] is a Jungian construct (Abrams & Zweig, 1991; Henderson, 1990; Jung, 1953). It is essentially the repressed, suppressed, and unwanted aspects of ourselves. Generally, it is unconscious and is projected onto others through judgments. People who practice consensual BDSM have self-reported that pain and/or control surface these hidden and repressed personal inner issues and facilitate their integration. The following section explores the nature of transformative pain and the ways in which BDSM relationships can form a container for depth psychological transformation.

Pain Reframed

> When I am shivering in my bones from fear, I am alive; when I hear myself screaming knowing I am not the feeling or the thought, I am alive. When I experience the burning sting from the whip, it hurts, but, I am also connected to my Master's will; my body stops being mine as I yield my will, and starts to dance to his call as I consciously let go control, feel the feelings and thoughts but release them to the place between us. Each sting keeps me present, in the now; each cut is his passionate kiss, each mark a symbol of his love. My heart fills with gratitude. I dance and sway to the rhythm, his music, his will transplanted over mine is grace; allows me to surrender. In that surrender I fall into nothing and in nothing, I find all. Ecstasy and devotion overflow in my heart. I am deeply grateful to him. (Interview, slave C, February 2004)

By being consensually and consciously present and embodied in the suffering, an alchemical reaction occurs for both sadist and masochist. If one merely focused on understanding the sensation, one runs the risk of concretizing the phenomena, reducing it into a caricature, and missing the deeper spiritual and metaphorical meanings of surrender, yielding, sacrificing, and serving inherent in letting go of ego.

To provide language for these transformative experiences, presenters of BDSM workshops have used spiritual and depth psychological constructs to describe the potential for sexual experiences and relationships to be a safe container for transformation and growth in individual, emotional, and spiritual ways (Sagarin et al., 2015; Shahbaz, 2009a). Raven Kaldera (2006) has written extensively about ordeal pain. He suggests pain can be used as a technique to achieve an altered state, to create energy, bring people back in touch with their bodies in the moment, and to serve as a sacrifice to a divine power.

In interviews of participants at the Dance of Souls[5] ritual, many described how the experiences were deeply healing and transformative. BDSM practitioners have reported that they believe physical pain is the fastest route to ensuring the mind stays in the moment. In the inescapable moment, the ego has to grapple with suffering without denial and avoidance, and what transpires is a breaking through, or falling into complete surrender.

"Cathartic flogging" is a term used by those in the BDSM community to describe the emotional release obtained by masochists from flogging. In workshops, BDSM practitioners explain how the intentional use of intense rhythmic sensation breaks down psychological defenses of strongly and deeply guarded emotions. By doing so these highly protected emotions surface into conscious experience such that they can be "metabolized" or processed from an embodied state.

Box 7.1 Interview Comments from Dance of Souls Participants, (Shahbaz, 2010)

"I feel a freedom, it is joyful, love, freely expressed love in a context of a lack of self-consciousness. Freedom from fear of how I am perceived." (slave R, interview, March, 2009)

"I had been very depressed prior to the dance and had truly questioned whether continuing with my life was worth it. I had to face that moment of saying YES again to Spirit, to the contract we had both entered into a long long time ago. I got lots of loving and felt a calm afterwards." (slave K, interview, March, 2009)

"Once the piercing was done I felt angry with the lupus. Suddenly my experience became about the lupus as if it was a person I wanted to kill. The lupus stole the enjoyment of the pain. I felt pissed. So I was processing that." (slave D, interview, March, 2009)

"I knew how powerful those tools are to opening to have different mystical experiences. And I wanted to show myself I could do this despite my fear of it. I didn't want to let my fears stop me" (Master C, interview February, 2009)

"Because there was so much pain I focused on the pain, and I started laughing, because I had an 'aha' moment. The 'aha' was that it doesn't matter about losing the ability to feel the pleasure in the pain, and not being able to take pain anymore, it doesn't matter, there are people who are starving, suffering, animals going through vivisection, my suffering is nothing compared to others. So I can't be a pain pig anymore it doesn't matter. Then something Jan used to say me came back to me like a mantra, let it be. The laughing turned into crying, I was able to just let it go." (slave D, interview, March, 2009)

I don't know at what stage I just went into bliss (subspace) – I could feel my eyes roll up in my head and I could see the purple light, I felt bliss-ful and didn't want to come back. I was the last person they unhooked. R came over and walked me to the piercing station to be unhooked. I remember being so blissed I had "kriyas" [ecstatic spiritual experience] shaking through my body for at least five hours afterwards. (Interview, Master D, February 2009)

Thus, BDSM done consciously has the potential to transform hidden and repressed feelings that depth psychology refers to as shadow work (Abrams & Zweig, 1991). BDSM practitioners are consciously using pain as psycho-spiritual transformative practice. This practice entails within it a safe con-tainer, which includes a trusted individual to whom one can surrender while intentionally pushing oneself beyond one's emotional or physical comfort limits (Lex, 1976). Through the interplay of pain (suffering) and pleasure, people describe "being taken out of themselves" and into intense embod-ied experiences. They additionally report intensification and amplification of their experience from the controlled pain, situating one in the present, in the body and yet transcending it.

Therapeutic Relationship Container

The authors have observed two forms of transformative relationship in con-sensual BDSM. The first entails using either pain play or a power-exchange relationship as a container to create safety and structure for individuals managing different forms of mental illness. The second entails dynam-ics that enable individuals to develop and/or grow psychologically or spiritually.

SM is sacred work for me, and the product or benefit for me is the quality of the interaction of the two people doing it. For me it is a relationship – in a particular its structure. SM is not a transaction for me or a substitute for analysis; it's a way of deepening self through a primal metaphysical and mythic relationship. (Interview, slave H, August 2009)

This journey is metaphorically about the unknown. We/i[6] am doing things and going places where very few go and therefore, the number of people with whom i can discuss or share this with is very lim-ited. At home i don't have people i can connect with. Connection and dialogue is central to my ability to reflect and assimilate these new experiences into an increased awareness of who i am and can't really be done separate from or outside the very M/s relationship. (Interview, slave S, April 2006)

The container and structure functions of transformative relationship dynamics are reiterated by individual self-reports of practitioners of BDSM practices and are widely discussed at BDSM events. In the following sections we will explore how BDSM relationships can form containers for deeper insight and growth as well as provide containment for dealing with mental, emotional, or physical disabilities. Some of these discussions are of pertinent interest to psychological theories.

Container for Deeper Insight and Growth

Exploring and processing embodied experiences elicited through BDSM practice can be approached only in relation with another. BDSM relationships entail enormous mutual trust. This deep sense of partnership enables inner tensions to be acknowledged as well as explored utilizing an experiential rather than a language-based process common to mainstream psychotherapy, which predominately focuses on cognitive processing as a means to problem resolution. For example, inner conflicts may exist between what the submissive wants and what the Dominant wants. These oppositional interpersonal tensions provide opportunity for insight into personal fears and blockages, which in turn result in an expansion of self-awareness and awareness of the other in relation.

This transformative relationship dynamic, which may be unique to BDSM, also reinforces deep questions about the nature of being, which is a spiritual/ existential query, as new insights emerge. These aspects are reflected in these comments from practitioners of BDSM:

This is not a solo journey. When i do edge stuff with Master, go into places i know not many others go – i can't go there alone, i need to feel connected in order to be able to experience meaning through my relationship to my Master as slave. (Interview, slave T, August 2009)

One's sense of self is intensified and expanded, the potential meaning of one's slavery and Mastery is enlarged. Thus the construct of the Master slave relationship allows for trust to occur in which sadomasochistic practices can be used as a tool by which to explore deeper depth psychological issues individually and in relationship. (Interview, Master D, August 2009)

For me, the way to go to deeper is to experience the journey in connection with my Master – i process the SM through the quality and depth of the connection. In this, the meaning imbued in the relationship fuels my purpose. Being travelers together on this journey deepens Our/our connection – bonding – relationship – union – link. This connection is vital to me as it serves both the metaphorical vehicle through which i can make the journey, and the medium through which i can process and learn about the depth of being slave. (Interview, slave H, August 2009)

Container for Mental, Emotional, and Physical Disabilities

It is commonly understood in psychotherapeutic practice that predictability and daily structure support the stabilization of psychiatric disabilities. The authors contend the structure inherent in BDSM relationships, in particular long-term M/s dynamics, can similarly provide a container for mental, emotional, and physical disabilities. It is important to state that the implementation of these types of structure within BDSM relationships is not a substitution for professional assessment and ongoing treatment. The following ethnographic autobiographical self-reports by individuals within the BDSM outline how these structures can facilitate stability in alternative relationships where one or both partners have a disability.

Practitioners of BDSM speak at length about the transformative benefits of BDSM practices and relationships with mental health problems, specifically, depression, obsessive-compulsive disorders, and Asperger's Syndrome.[7] Raven Kaldera and Del Tashlin wrote two books – an anthology, *Broken Toys: Submissives with Mental Illness or Neurological Disorders* (2013a) and *Mastering Mind: Dominants with Mental Illness or Neurological Disorders* (2013b) – specifically related to submissives and Dominants with mental illness, providing excellent phenomenological information. These anthologies are highly valuable for both professionals and individuals who attempt power-exchange relationships while managing their psychiatric and neurological challenges. The following sections will discuss several examples using ethnographic phenomenological reports from people within the BDSM community who have chosen to come and speak up about their experiences.

Master DK and slave T: Dealing with Clinical Depression

Master DK and slave T came out to their BDSM community to discuss how to use an M/s relationship to assist in the management of clinical depression.

Slave T is clinically diagnosed with depression. As part of his responsibility in the relationship, Master DK devised a structure utilizing control that created a responsible and beneficial container for management of his slave's depression. This was developed through consultation with slave T's psychiatric care provider. Master DK established house rules and protocols around his compliance with prescribed therapeutic interventions. Slave T's compliance with Master DK's protocol was reframed and defined as service to his Master opposed to independently directed self-care. The protocol involved slave T's compliance with treatment recommendations (i.e., medication adherence, psychotherapy) as well as having to communicate his inner state as opposed to withholding his feelings from his Master. As a result, Master DK and slave T were able to lessen the severity and frequency of depressive episodes. Additionally, Master DK required acts of service to the household as a method of creating and maintaining slave T's purpose and importance in the relationship.

Master K and boy J: Managing Asperger's

Similarly, Master K and boy J have conducted educational forums describing how they use obedience and control dynamics with respect to boy J being clinically diagnosed with Asperger's Disorder. Their experience and recommendations using a structured power-exchange relationship as a way to provide a supportive container for a partner with mild ASD (Autistic Spectrum Disorder), as well as the experiences of similar individuals, is chronicled in the previously mentioned anthologies by Kaldera and Tashlin (2013a, 2013b).

Master F and slave E: Bipolar Disorder

Both Master F and slave E have Bipolar Disorder, Type II; ADD; anxiety as well as obsessive-compulsive symptoms. Both take medication and define specific protocols for slave E in the event Master F is psychiatrically impaired. She states, "We have ordered E to disobey any orders that obviously come from a place that does not offer good stewardship; for example, if we were to become extremely unbalanced. We feel comfortable knowing that E could make a decision about Our health, and do what is necessary in order to get Us treatment if We were not mentally able to do that for Ourselves" (Kaldera & Tashlin, 2013a, p. 19). Slave E notes that his ability to obey this specific protocol is predicated on his own mental and emotional clarity. His sense of serving his Master enables him to do what is necessary at the time. However, he notes, it is fortunate that "when one of us is out of sorts, the other is usually more stable at the time. It is rare that we are both lacking in mood stability simultaneously" (p. 20).

In 2015, both Master F and slave E had concurrent bipolar episodes. During this time, Master F suspended her slave's compliance with all protocols, enabling each of them to focus entirely on their respective treatment. It is notable that during this suspended period slave E was admitted to an inpatient psychiatric treatment center. This decision indicates judicious and conscious discernment of when, and when not, to use M/s protocols as a therapeutic adjunct. They describe this decision as exemplifying an act of compassion, which is a fundamental aspect and guiding principle of their ongoing spiritual practice. Their practice of compassion is fundamental to their Master/slave dynamics, rituals, and protocols.

These ethnographic self-reports provide psychotherapists insights into how to incorporate the control/obedience dynamic in BDSM relationships as a therapeutic construct that does not replace but supports formal therapy and clinical interventions. Neurological or emotional disabilities that require boundary-setting, such as depression, ASD, and obsessive-compulsive disorders, can benefit from the predictable structure of power-exchange relationships. Some speakers and writers within the community have cautioned about conflating therapy with the therapeutic aspects of BDSM relationships (Shahbaz, 2008, 2009b, 2012b). They seek to clarify that these nontraditional relationships are not a replacement for therapy but can, however, have therapeutic outcomes if engaged in with conscious intent and other noted characteristics in this book.

It is particularly the consensual and conscious control and structure inherent in these dynamics that enables a supportive and loving relationship environment, within which healthy emotional and behavioral boundaries are established and reinforced. Within a committed, consensual relationship, the addition of these elements provides a therapeutic element for a variety of disabilities.

Kink-aware psychiatrist Dr. Sabrina Popp, co-editor of *Unequal by Design: Counseling Power Dynamic Relationships – A Manual by and for Mental Health Professionals*, has found these relationships to be an advantage in getting clients to follow their therapeutic protocols. She writes:

> For example, if a submissive or slave is having trouble doing some of the activities I want them to do in order to help them to get healthy, the master can step in. Perhaps they can get rewards for it if they do it properly, or perhaps the master will just tell them that they have to do it for their own health and for the stress level of the master, too. So invoking the relationship can make the submissive or slave more motivated to do what they have to because it makes the relationship stronger.

By the same token, when it's the dominant who has the problem, the submissive needs to be empowered enough to say, "What service can I do to help you follow these instructions? How can I make it as easy and painless as possible? If you're having trouble getting out of bed in the morning, what can I do to make that process easier for you?" They can also bring up the point that "I need you to be healthy because you're my master and I am depending on you to direct me, so I need you to do your best to get healthy." It's the counterpart of the master saying, "Your service is an important part of my life, and you can't be of service to me unless you get better, so I am very invested in you getting better." These can be really powerful motivations, but first you have to go to the trouble of getting the partner comfortable with you, the therapist. Once you have them on board, you can do a lot more. (Kaldera & Popp, 2014)

Understanding the therapeutic value of these relationships provides therapists non-psychological frameworks and constructs as a supportive adjunct during therapy processes with their clients. Therapists are encouraged to explore their client's house rules and protocols to explore individualized approaches for this purpose and to evaluate ancillary community supports if both, the Master and slave, have similar or co-occurring mental health diagnoses needing support and structure. Non-kink-aware professional therapists working with this specific scenario are further encouraged to seek clinical supervision for working with these clients from an ethically appropriate and culturally sensitive framework.

Transformative Authenticity

Connecting and belonging to community can be transformative for people with atypical sexuality, who often experience alienation. Being with like-minded people is validating and affirming, which additionally consolidates personal identity. The result is often a sense of authenticity. Clarity about self and self-acceptance are important aspects of psychotherapy with BDSM clients. Understanding the interrelationship between affirming community and authentic self-expression is an important aspect of psychotherapy with BDSM clients to ensure they are connected to a community, whenever possible.

There are a number of annual events that draw people from around the world to connect, share, and learn from one another. These events, in the words of a regular attendee, have become the equivalent of what Greenwich Village in New York City was to the gay community in the 1970s. These events are where people who practice BDSM go to build community, be affirmed, and confirmed. While these events draw new attendees, they also draw together a high percentage of regular attendees. People celebrate new relationships, build new friendships, and commemorate those who have passed.

The Southwest Leather Conference and its signature event, the Dance of Souls ritual, provide exactly that container in which meaning is ascribed for both the individual and the collective. The power involved in the hook pull enables individuals to draw power from the collective strength or identity to support the ordeal journey for their own individuation process (Sagarin et al., 2015; Vale & Juno, 1989). In turn, the process works on and is in turn amplified by the collective consciousness of the BDSM tribe (Shahbaz, 2009b, 2010).

What was universally acknowledged and understood from the authors' personal interviews conducted with various participants at the Dance of Souls was the transformative healing and connection with spiritual aspects of the ritual. People reported seeing visions and hearing inner voices, and allowed themselves to be open to possibilities beyond their conscious will. At the same time, they reported experiences of connection to their own BDSM tribe, people like themselves.

> It was a singular experience; others were dancing with others. For me it was a singular experience surrounded by my tribe. Alone with myself, but in the presence of my family and extended tribe. Strange and wonderful experience. (Interview, Master C, February 2009)

> Dance of Souls serves the Leather community in providing a venue, a space, for people to experience all the many facets of themselves in a context that many may feel comfortable – S/m. Looking at the Divine within you while doing something that you're already comfortable with makes it easier. (Interview, slave K, March 2009)

> There was a tribal community feeling and a connection to a tribal self. I am generally a loner. Being there [in the Dance of Souls] feels open, radiant, communal – there is a feeling of at-one-ness, a joyfulness to it. There is a full-out expression that is no-holds-back. There is a type of eye contact I would not have otherwise engaged in – a very intense eye contact with a lack of self-consciousness. (Interview, slave R, March 2009)

Feelings of being held, contained, validated, and accepted were continuously expressed as an important and valued part of their experiences. A three-time participant at the Dance of Souls poignantly describes how she experienced this collective consciousness from the first time:

Doing something that you're already comfortable with makes it easier. (Interview, slave K, March 2009)

The Dance of Souls ritual and other collective practices enable people to learn to trust that they can let go of ego, if only for a moment, and is akin to group or team skill-building in corporate settings. When confronted by life-altering events, this is a useful skill to have – to let go and trust in a higher power, or at least in one's own ability to move gracefully with challenging situations.

When my reputation was publicly trashed and I was scapegoated online I didn't fall apart, and I didn't react with revenge or attack back. I think the reason was because I do SM and I knew I could trust in a higher power, I knew I was internally resilient and strong. Doing SM has made me in ways I could never imagine a more stronger person. (Interview, slave T, March 2009).

All those interviewed stressed the critical importance of connection with friends, family of choice, and the tribe for support and love during and after the dance.

So much stuff came up for me that I couldn't contain. I went to my room and howled out all the pain. I knew it was okay and that I was releasing lots of stuff from my previous relationship but, it took me a while to calm down. It wasn't until friends came looking for me that I felt able to let go completely. They were fantastic, wouldn't leave me alone till I was okay. (Interview, slave K, March 2009)

Through ethnographic reports and personal interviews, it appears this collective healing experienced by individuals in a supportive and loving way is a critical element of the positive empowering process of the Dance of Souls. These individual experiences are similar to those described in traditional shamanic rituals. They have an extended impact on a person's sense of self and identity, and oftentimes appear to be catalytic transformational forces. People consciously face their own fears and move through them in the loving support of their community.

Psychotherapists need to appreciate the invaluable value connection to community provides. When consciously engaging in sadomasochistic practices, new insights reinforce and deepen meaning. The sense of individual transformation, lives changing, and increasing awareness of self are evident in individual practices as well as in people experiencing the Dance of Souls for the first time (or multiple times). The loving and supportive nature of BDSM dynamics and/or the BDSM community – of which the Dance of Souls is an example – seems to provide a catalytic process in which transformative healing can take place. It enhances participants' sense of identity and gives them the experience of belonging to a wider loving and supportive tribe.

In Summary

The opportunity to explore the transformative aspects of BDSM are only just slowly starting to emerge through ethnographic reports, depth psychological constructs, and psychobiological research into BDSM practices.

However, in order to appreciate this transformative function, psychotherapy must conceptualize and form a very different relationship with the human experience of suffering. Professional counselors and therapists need to reframe suffering from a question of "whether to suffer" to "how to suffer." James Hillman has argued that by not needing to "fix" things, we are free to treat suffering as a source of purpose and meaning (Hillman, 1975). This paradigmatic shift allows psychotherapy to engage with transformative pain rather than suppress, dismiss, or otherwise ignore pain.

BDSM practice is not therapy, but it has potential to be deeply therapeutic. As the above discussions indicate, BDSM can be a useful adjunct when used with consciousness and awareness of symptoms. In particular, the use of orders, protocols, and service to provide structure, containment, and purpose is invaluable. Without pathologizing this atypical sexuality, professional counselors may clarify, enhance, and/or assist in creating language for embodied experiences and insights.

The authors call upon further research to examine the efficacy of BDSM as an adjunct to psychotherapy.

Notes

1 Experiential body workers also include the fields of sexological bodywork, sacred intimacy, massage therapy, and psychodrama, among others. The overarching client goal is to teach and learn how to listen to the knowledge within the body and understand the psychological/emotional connection among the mind, body, and spirit. By doing so clients are able to obtain an embodied emotional awareness and understanding that is deeper than a cerebral/intellectual understanding that arises through talk therapy.
2 See Knight (2014) for a detailed explanation of somatic embodied phenomenon and its role in meaning making.
3 See Grof (2008) for a discussion on the history of transperonal psychology.
4 Swiss Psychologist Carl Jung described the shadow as "that hidden, repressed, for the most part inferior and guilt-laden personality whose ultimate ramifications reach back into the realm of our animal ancestors ... If it has been believed hitherto that the human shadow was the source of evil, it can now be ascertained on closer

investigation that the unconscious man, that is his shadow does not consist only of morally reprehensible tendencies, but also displays a number of good qualities, such as normal instincts, appropriate reactions, realistic insights, creative impulses etc." [CW9 paras 422 & 423]. All that we ascribe as unacceptable, evil, inferior, and repress in ourselves becomes a part of the shadow. When it is continually repressed, it is thought to manifest in psychological disturbance, including hositility, projection, and neurosis (Abrams, & Zweig, 1991; Henderson, 1990; Jung, Read, Fordham & Adler, 1953).

5 These interviews were conducted in 2009 by Caroline Shahbaz as part of her doctoral program. The Dance of Souls was first established in 2003, with a conscious and deliberate intention to create a shamanic healing experience by the founders of South West Leather Conference (SWLC), Master Steve Sampson and his slave, Kirk. Master Steve Sampson self-identifies as a sadomasochistic Master and practicing Buddhist monk. His slave, Kirk, identifies as a masochistic slave and is the National Arch-Druid of the American Druidic Association. As a result of the founders' different psycho-spiritual backgrounds, their experience with sadomasochistic practices, acquaintance with Fakir Musafar (http:// www.fakir.org), and participation in his "Spirit and Flesh Ecstatic Shamanism" workshops and rituals (http://www.fakir.org/spiritflesh/index.html), they were able to conceive a fit between the shamanic rituals and practices involving physical pain and suffering with certain sadomasochistic practices that, when combined, would result in a powerful and relevant passage for healing in the BDSM community. On an individual basis, the quintessential power in the Dance of Souls is the capacity for this ritual to create a pathway to what Jung called "individuation." Since the first hook pull of the Dance of Souls at SWLC in 2003, hundreds of people have participated, and the majority return each year to undergo this ordeal path again.

6 In the Master slave culture small "i" is often used by the person who identifies as slave, and capital letter "I" refers to a Master. This is a form of written protocol required by some Master slave pairs. In reporting on the ethnographic interviews and correspondences with slaves and Masters known to follow this cultural protocol, the authors have attempted to keep their preferred Master slave etiquette in transcribing their spoken and written narration.

7 Asperger's Disorder was recently reclassified in the DSM-5 as Autism Spectrum Disorder (ASD). See *American Psychiatric Association Diagnostic and Statistical Manual of Mental Disorders, Fifth Edition.*

Appendix A: Shahbaz-Chirinos Healthy BDSM Checklist

As we have previously explored, engaging in or wanting to engage in BDSM is not a sign of mental illness, weakness, or pathology. However, because it is a marginalized community, it is a demographic that is open to predators and frauds who prey on the naïve and uneducated. The authors developed the *Shahbaz-Chirinos Healthy BDSM Checklist* to assist professional counselors in determining whether their clients are practicing constructive BDSM. This checklist was developed in relation to people in the BDSM community and encompasses a wide range of issues addressed in this handbook. Predominantly, its primary aim is to explore (1) whether clients are engaging in BDSM consensually; (2) to assist clients in obtaining clarity about their reason, vision, and philosophy of the practice of BDSM; and (3) the degree to which their values align with their practices. Lastly, the Shahbaz-Chirinos Healthy BDSM Checklist is designed to clarify if the client has developed a culturally appropriate and consistent process that supports his relationship choices.

The checklist reminds therapists to determine whether BDSM is part of the client's identity or simply a relatively minor aspect of his sexual exploration and repertoire. Further, it assists therapists in clarifying their clients' ability to build culturally appropriate and consistent systems and infrastructure to support their relationship choices. It focuses therapist questions that discern culturally appropriate knowledge and skills about BDSM and whether clients are actively connected to a BDSM community for support. Ultimately, this checklist seeks to discern whether clients exhibit a positive sense of expansion and well-being as a result of engaging in BDSM.

Table A.1 Shahbaz-Chirinos Healthy BDSM Behavior Checklist

Key Area	What to Explore	Questions to Ask Clients	Clinical Indications of Problematic BDSM Behavior	Therapeutic Approaches/ Intervention
		What is your understanding about consensual BDSM?	Lack of consent is a concern and possibly an indicator of abuse.	Explore the lack of consent. Establish mutually agreed consent. Educate, if necessary, and connect your clients to a BDSM community.
		Have you discussed issues about consent with your BDSM partners?		
		How do you define consent in your relationship?	Lack of a process to develop and maintain ethical responsibility and support may be an indication of intimate partner abuse (domestic violence).	
		How do you practice consensual BDSM?		
Consent	Verify your clients engage in BDSM consensually.	Do changes made within the relationship dynamics require the consent of all the partners regardless of their roles?		Educate clients about parameters and type of consent (overt vs. covert) as well as expectations resulting from an impending scene or prospective/current relationship.
		Can you choose to leave this relationship? If so, what types of support and barriers are in place for this process?		
		Does the dominant party in a power exchange relationship demonstrate an ethical responsible approach to those under their authority?		

Key Area	What to Explore	Questions to Ask Clients	Clinical Indications of Problematic BDSM Behavior	Therapeutic Approaches/ Intervention
	Evidence for personal inner well-being, personal growth, increased sense of competency and/or spiritual evolution – especially in the submissive or slave in a D/s or M/s relationship.	Do you feel respected and valued as a result of engaging in BDSM?	Low sense of personal well-being or personal growth may be indicative of a client seeking affirmation over expressing his true identity and BDSM desires (identity/expression incongruence).	Check to see whether your client(s) have a psychiatric diagnosis by referring to a psychiatrist and obtaining collateral information when indicated.
Wellness		Do you feel a sense of expansion and well-being as a result of engaging in BDSM?		
		What plans (physical, psychological, financial) have been put in place in the event this relationship ends?		
	The existence of your clients' awareness and utilization of culturally appropriate values; e.g., SSC and RACK.	To what extent are your values centered on monogamy and equality?	Lack of clarity can lead to inconsistent behaviors and send confused messages.	Explore and assist clients to clarify for themselves issues related to ethics, responsibility to self and other, and culturally appropriate values.
		Are you aware of culturally appropriate values such as safe, sane, and consensual and Risk-Aware Consensual Kink?		
Values		How do your personal values inform your beliefs and practice of consensual non-monogamy and unequal power relationship dynamics?		
		Is there an openness to learn and develop self-awareness, skills, and personal growth?		
		Is there an openness to explore alternative relationship models?		

(continued)

Table A.1 Shahbaz-Chirinos Healthy BDSM Behavior Checklist (*continued*)

Key Area	What to Explore	Questions to Ask Clients	Clinical Indications of Problematic BDSM Behavior	Therapeutic Approaches/ Intervention
		How do you interpret and practice culturally appropriate values such as honor, integrity, responsibility, and honesty?	Lack of congruence can lead to feelings of inauthenticity, confusion, and inconsistent behaviors.	Help your client(s) clarify their values and align their behaviors with these values.
		What values do you profess to live by, and how do you demonstrate these?		
Walking the Talk	Congruence between values and behavioral dynamics of the relationship.	Does the Dominant partner in a D/s or M/s relationship demonstrate an ethical responsible approach to his slave(s)?		Practice consistent congruity by helping client(s) reframe and make meaning through establishing symbolisms and rituals in their relationship.
		If there is an authority exchange, does the Dominant partner follow the advice they give to others?		
		How do you practice activities that lead to growth?		

Key Area	What to Explore	Questions to Ask Clients	Clinical Indications of Problematic BDSM Behavior	Therapeutic Approaches/ Intervention
		What are your expectations of a BDSM and/or kinky relationship?	Lack of clarity about why they are in a BDSM relationship can lead to inconsistencies, difficulty forming relationships, and struggles in relationships.	Help your client(s) clarify and articulate why they are in or want to be in a BDSM relationship.
	Extent of consciousness regarding	Can you articulate why you practice BDSM or why you are in a BDSM relationship?		
Clarity	purpose, vision, or philosophy about their relationship.	If there is an authority exchange, how does the Dominant partner demonstrate an ethical and responsible approach to managing his slave(s)?		Encourage your client(s) to clarify each person's place in polydynamic relationship structures.
		To what degree are you monogamous or polygamous? **If in a kinky and polyamorous relationship:** How is the polyamorous relationship structured?	Lack of clarity about one's place in a polydynamic can lead to insecurity, jealousy, and envy.	
		What are your expectations of a BDSM, kinky, and poly relationship?		

(continued)

Table A.1 Shahbaz-Chirinos Healthy BDSM Behavior Checklist (*continued*)

Key Area	What to Explore	Questions to Ask Clients	Clinical Indications of Problematic BDSM Behavior	Therapeutic Approaches/ Intervention
		Why do you practice BDSM?	Being versus doing is central to the degree of psychological isolation and alienation that might be experienced.	If one is less identified than the other, help your client(s) understand the difficulties they may encounter and help your client(s) reach alignment.
		Why are you in (or want to be in) a BDSM relationship?		
		Is the BDSM interest/relationship a core part of your identity or is it limited to sexual exploration?		
		How does BDSM define your identity?	In a relationship, look for misalignment between the couple's identity.	
	Is BDSM part of their sexual identity or only an aspect of their sexual exploration and repertoire?	Do you bracket BDSM as part of your sexual expression? To what degree are you monogamous or polygamous?		For clients who derive identity from BDSM, ensure they are networked with appropriate communities.
Identity		Why are you in a BDSM relationship?		
		How do you define your sexual identity?		
		How have you (couple/ individual) reflected on your sexual identity? What insights have you drawn from this reflection?		
		Is BDSM part of your sexual identity? If so, how important is it to you in your relationship?		
		Is BDSM broadly or specifically part of your sexual repertoire?		

Key Area	What to Explore	Questions to Ask Clients	Clinical Indications of Problematic BDSM Behavior	Therapeutic Approaches/Intervention
	Explore evidence of culturally appropriate knowledge and skills about the practical application of BDSM as well as BDSM relationship skills.	How have you developed your BDSM physical skills? (Workshops, mentors, books, videos?) How have you developed your relationship skills to be in an authority exchange, kinky, and/or polyamorous relationship?	Lack of skills indicates a higher potential for unsafe BDSM practices.	Help your clients connect to BDSM groups and resources to develop skills and knowledge.
Skills & Knowledge		Relative to your practice, how do you (person or couple) define and practice safe BDSM? Have you attended workshops on how to develop BDSM skills? Which ones? Have you attended workshops to develop BDSM relationship skills? How have you developed your relationship skills to be in a kinky-poly relationship (communication pattern and style, etc.)?		

(continued)

Table A.1 Shahbaz-Chirinos Healthy BDSM Behavior Checklist (*continued*)

Key Area	What to Explore	Questions to Ask Clients	Clinical Indications of Problematic BDSM Behavior	Therapeutic Approaches/ Intervention
Clear Relationship Structures	Evidence of culturally appropriate relationship structure to support their relationship choices (rituals, rules, and protocols).	What is the purpose of the relationship and how have you incorporated it (verbal, written) into your rituals, rules? What are the rituals and protocols you have put in place in this relationship and why? What is the relevance of the rituals, protocols, and structures in your BDSM relationship? How do you reflect on and review your relationship structures? If this relationship is a poly situation, how is it structured? In a kinky and poly relationship, what boundaries have been put in place to ensure each participant has a clear and respected place?	Poor or lack of appropriate supportive rituals, rules, and protocols can indicate poorly thought-through or immature authority exchange dynamics, which can contribute to anxiety, confusion, and conflict in relationships.	Help your client(s) understand the importance of building and supporting sound culturally appropriate relationship structures, rituals, and rules (protocols). Encourage them to connect to educational BDSM groups.

Key Area	What to Explore	Questions to Ask Clients	Clinical Indications of Problematic BDSM Behavior	Therapeutic Approaches/ Intervention
Dyadic Communication and Problem-Solving Processes	Evidence of consistent communication processes, especially around problem solving that supports their relationship choices.	What mechanisms have each of you established in your relationship to identify and deal with problems in the relationship? Are the established communication protocols effectively allowing each of you to express your opinions, desires, and needs? How effectively do you (individuals or couple) identify and work through shame and guilt in your relationship? What do you do to deal with interpersonal conflict or disagreements?	Lack of appropriate communication and conflict/ problem-solving create problems in relationship dynamics.	Help your client(s) build effective two-way communication and problem-solving processes.

(continued)

Table A.1 Shahbaz-Chirinos Healthy BDSM Behavior Checklist (*continued*)

Key Area	What to Explore	Questions to Ask Clients	Clinical Indications of Problematic BDSM Behavior	Therapeutic Approaches/ Intervention
		Are you out of the closet to your family and friends?	Isolation contributes to alienation, depression, lack of skills development, and/or refinement, which may increase unforeseen risk.	Encourage your clients to seek out and connect to real-life BDSM groups and communities.
		Do you have friendship networks who know about their BDSM interests and relationship? Are these networks online or in real life?		
Supportive community	Is there support from friends, family (chosen or biological), and/or a supportive connection to a BDSM community?	In long-term authority exchange relationships, has the dominant partner made medical, legal, supportive arrangements to care for their submissive/slave?		
		Do you have a network of kink-aware medical professionals, particularly as it pertains to scenes that may go awry or have an unexpected outcome?		
		Are you connected to real people in the BDSM community?		
		Do you have supportive friends or mentors in the BDSM community?		

Appendix B: NCSF's Annual Incident Reporting

The following table is collated from the National Coalition for Sexual Freedom (NCSF) Incident Reporting and Response annual reports, available online at www.ncsfreedom.org. Refer to the NCSF website for more details at https://ncsfreedom.org/key-programs/incident-response/incident-response.html.

Table B.1 Information Collated from NCSF's Incident Reporting and Response Annual Reports

Year	Statistics*
2002	600 requests for information and assistance. Largest category was child custody and divorce cases. Job discrimination, 12 incidents. Criminal cases, 4 incidents. Media incidents, 81 interviews given, Jack McGeorge, media training. Kink clubs, police raids.
2003	Over 500 requests for information and assistance. Largest category was child custody and divorce cases. Rise in employment discrimination, 20 incidents. Criminal cases.
2004	Over 740 requests for information and assistance. Largest category was child custody and divorce cases. Rise in criminal and legal issues.
2005	Over 700 requests for information and assistance. 58% BDSM related. 31% referrals for criminal, divorce custody. 15% custody divorce related. Increase in criminal. Increase in employment discrimination.

(*continued*)

Table B.1 Information Collated from NCSF's Incident Reporting and Response
Annual Reports (*continued*)

Year	Statistics*
2006	73.5% BDSM issues An increase in criminal and domestic violence. Increase in employment discrimination. • 19% child custody and divorce (13.5% were regarding child custody/divorce issues and 5.5% were in reference to child protective services' complaints). • 14.5% were related to SM/leather/fetish group issues. • 13% were requests regarding SM/abuse/domestic violence issues. • 7% were regarding employment discrimination.
2007	Not available.
2008	Processed 114 requests. 85.5% BDSM related. 31% child custody divorce issues. 27% regarding criminal issues. 15.5 BDSM group issues. An increase in criminal issues.
2009	95.5% BDSM issues. 36% criminal issues. 27.5% child custody and divorce issues. 17.5% BDSM groups. 11% SM abuse domestic violence issues.
2010	Not available.
2011	87% BDSM issues. 154 were related to SM/leather/fetish group issues. 135 were regarding criminal complaint issues. 112 were requests regarding SM/abuse/domestic violence/assault issues, including criminal complaints regarding consent and protective orders. 115 were regarding child custody/divorce issues. 27 were regarding employment discrimination.
2012	137 were requests regarding SM/abuse/domestic violence/assault issues, including criminal complaints regarding consent and protective orders. 76 were regarding criminal complaint issues. 14 were regarding employment discrimination. 87 were regarding child custody/divorce issues. 77 were related to SM/leather/fetish group issues.
2013	Not available.

Year	Statistics*
2014	73 criminal issues. 37 (33 child custody and 4 divorce). 26 requests for info from professionals. 20 kink group issues. A significant drop in child custody divorce issues in comparison to the previous reporting year.

Source: Wright, S. (2015). *NCSF Incident Reporting & Response Annual Report.* Retrieved from https://ncsfreedom.org/key-programs/incident-response/incident-response.html

Note

*Statistics are shown from the NCSF's website where they have been made available. Refer to the NCSF website for more details at https://ncsfreedom.org/key-programs/incident-response/incident-response.html.

Appendix C: BDSM Organizations and Resources

The following list of BDSM organizations, informational websites, and events is finite. It is presented to provide psychotherapists a starting point in referring their client(s) to groups and educational resources within the BDSM community.

Organizations

Avatar
http://www.avatarla.org/publicweb/

Black Rose
http://www.br.org/

BDSM Events Calendar
http://BDSMeventscalendar.com/

The Eulenspiegel Society (TES)
http://www.tes.org/

Leather Archives and Museum
http://www.leatherarchives.org/

Leather Alliance.org
http://leatheralliance.org/

Leather Heart Foundation
http://www.leatherheart.org/

SF Citadel
http://www.sfcitadel.org/

Masters and slaves together (MAsT)
http://www.mast.net/

Los Angeles Boys of Leather
http://www.labol.org/home.php

Los Angeles Leather Coalition
http://www.lalc.info/Welcome.html

Orange Coast Leather Assembly (OCLA)
www.ocla.org

Paddles
http://www.paddlesnyc.com/events.html

The Australian BDSM Information Site
http://www.ozabis.info/

The Eulenspiegel Society
http://www.tes.org/

The Society of Janus
http://soj.org/

Threshold Society (Pansexual)
www.threshold.org

Informational Websites

Community Academic Consortium for Research on Alternative Sexualities
https://www.caras.ws/

Kink Aware Professionals (KAP)
http://www.ncsfreedom.org/index.php?option=com_keyword&id=270
http://www.bannon.com/kap/

Leather Archives Museum
http://www.leatherarchives.org/

Leatherati
http://www.leatherati.com/
http://www.leatherati.com/category/events/
http://www.leatherati.com/event/mtta-academy-female-slave-training-weekend/

Master/slave Development Center
http://www.msdevelopmentcenter.com/

National Coalition for Sexual Freedom (NCSF)
www.ncsfreedom.org

National Coalition Against Domestic Violence
http://www.uncfsp.org/projects/userfiles/file/dce-stop_now/ncadv_lgbt_
    fact_sheet.pdf

The Carter/Johnson Leather Library
http://www.leatherlibrary.org/home.html

Events (Educational)

Beat Me in St Louis
http://www.beatmeinstl.com/

Beyond Vanilla
http://beyondvanilla.org/

Black Beat
http://www.blackbeatinc.org/

Black Rose
http://www.br.org/br/index.php?

Bound in Boston
http://www.boundinboston.com/

Butchmanns Experience
http://www.butchmanns-experience.org/

Dark Odyssey
http://www.darkodyssey.com/landingPage.html

International Ms Leather
http://imsl.org/

Kinky Kollege
http://www.kinkykollege.com/

Find a Munch
http://findamunch.com/

Folsom Fringe SM Odyssey
http://folsomfringe.com/

International Mr. Leather
http://www.imrl.com/

International Ms Leather
http://www.imrl.com/

Leather HEAT
http://leatherheat.org/

Leather Leadership Conference
http://www.leatherleadership.org/

Leather Sir leather boy
http://www.ilsb-icbb.com/

Master/slave Conference
www.masterslaveconference.org

MTTA Academy
http://www.mtta.info/academy.html

Out of the Shadows: International Groups and Munches
http://www.sexuality.org/authors/lauren/IntGroups.html

Power Exchange Summit
http://www.powerexchangesummit.org/

South Plains Leatherfest
www.southplainsleatherfest.com

Southwest Leather Conference
www.southwestleather.org

Thunder in the Mountains
http://www.thunderinthemountains.com/

Northwest Leather Celebration
http://www.northwestleathercelebration.com/

References

Abrams, J., & Zweig, C. (1991). *Meeting the shadow: The hidden power of the dark side of human nature*. Los Angeles, CA: J.P. Tarcher.

Achola, A. J. (2014). *Porn: A very short look at society's relationship with pornography and its warped image of what is sexually morally right and wrong*. Booktango.

Allen, S. (2013). *Situating the controlled body: In cinema, pain and pleasure* (pp. 8– 25). Houndsmills: Palgrave Macmillan.

Ambler, J. K., Lee, E. M., Klement, K., R., Loewald, T., Comber, E. M., Hanson, S. A., Cutler, B., Cutler, N., & Sagarin, B. J. (in press). Consensual BDSM facilitates role-specific altered states of consciousness: A preliminary study. *Psychology of Consciousness: Theory, Research, and Practice*.

American Psychiatric Association (1987). *Diagnostic and statistical manual of mental disorders: DSM-III-R*. Washington, DC: American Psychiatric Association.

American Psychiatric Association (2013). *Diagnostic and statistical manual of mental disorders*. Fifth Edition. Arlington, VA: American Psychiatric Association.

Anderson, S. C. (1994). A critical analysis of the concept of codependency. *Social Work, 39*(6), 677–685.

Annon, J. S. (1976). The PLISSIT model: A proposed conceptual scheme for the behavioral treatment of sexual problems. *Journal of Sex Education and Therapy, 2*(1), 1–15.

Baldwin, G. (2002). *SlaveCraft: Roadmaps for consensual erotic servitude: Principles, skills, and tools*. Los Angeles, CA: Daedalus.

Baldwin, G., & Bean, J. W. (1993). *Ties that bind: The SM/leather/fetish erotic style: Issues, commentaries, and advice*. Los Angeles, CA: Daedalus.

Balsam, K. F., & Szymanski, D. M. (2005). Relationship quality and domestic violence in women's same-sex relationships: The role of minority stress. *Psychology of Women Quarterly, 29*(3), 258–269.

Bargh, J. A., & McKenna, K. Y. (2004). The Internet and social life. *Annu. Rev. Psychol., 55*, 573–590.

Barker, M. (2013). Consent is a grey area? A comparison of understandings of consent in *Fifty Shades of Grey* and on the BDSM blogosphere. *Sexualities, 16*(8), 896–914.

Barker, M., Iantaffi, A., & Gupta, C. (2007). Kinky clients, kinky counselling? The challenges and potentials of BDSM. In L. Moon (Ed.), *Feeling queer or queer feelings: Radical approaches to counselling sex, sexualities and genders* (pp. 106– 124). London, UK: Routledge.

Barker, M., & Langdridge, D. (2010). Whatever happened to non-monogamies? Critical reflections on recent research and theory. *Sexualities, 13*(6), 748–772.

Baumeister, R. F. (1997). The enigmatic appeal of sexual masochism: Why people desire pain, bondage, and humiliation sex. *Journal of Social and Clinical Psychology, 16*(2), 133.

Baumeister, R. F., & Butler, J. L. (1997). Sexual masochism: Deviance without pathology. In D. R. Laws & W. O'Donohue (Eds.), *Sexual deviance* (pp. 225–239). New York, NY: Guilford Press.

Bayer, R. (1987). *Homosexuality and american psychiatry: The politics of diagnosis.* Princeton, NJ: Princeton University Press.

Bean, J. W. (1994). *Leathersex: A guide for the curious outsider and the serious player.* Los Angeles, CA: Daedalus.

Beattie, M. (2013), *Codependent no more: How to stop controlling others and start caring for yourself.* Center City, MN: Hazelden.

Beckmann, A. (2008). The 'bodily practices' of consensual 'SM,' spirituality and 'transcendence.' In D. Langdridge, M. Barker (Eds.), *Safe, sane and consensual: Contemporary perspectives on sadomasochism* (pp. 98–118). Houndmills: Palgrave MacMillan.

Bennett, T. (2013). Sadomasochism under the human rights (sexual conduct) Act 1994. *Sydney Law Review, 35*, 541.

Benz, M. O., & Benz, M. O. (2015). Practitioners of BDSM found to be psychologically healthy. *Medicalresearch.com | Medical Research Interviews and News*, December 4. Retrieved from http://medicalresearch.com/?s=Practitioners+of+BDSM+found+to+be+psychologically&submit=Search.

Bezreh, T., Edgar, T., & Weinberg, T. (2012) BDSM disclosure and stigma management: Identifying opportunities for sex education. *American Journal of Sexuality Education, 7*(1), 37–61.

Bienvenu, R. V. (1998). *The development of sadomasochism as a cultural style in the twentieth-century United States.* (Unpublished doctoral dissertation). Indiana University, IN.

Billedo, C. J., Kerkhof, P., & Finkenauer, C. (2015). The use of social networking sites for relationship maintenance in long-distance and geographically close romantic relationships. *Cyberpsychology, Behavior, and Social Networking, 18*(3), 152–157.

Bohus, M., Limberger, M., Ebner, U., Glocker, F. X., Schwarz, B., Wernz, M., & Lieb, K. (2000). Pain perception during self-reported distress and calmness in patients with borderline personality disorder and self-mutilating behavior. *Psychiatry Research, 95*, 251–260. Retrieved from http://dx.doi.org/10.1016/S0165-1781(00)00179-7.

Bourget, D., & Gagné, P. (2012). Women who kill their mates. *Behavioral Sciences & the Law, 30*(5), 598–614. doi:10.1002/bsl.2033.

Braun-Harvey, D., & Vigorito, M. A. (2016). *Treating out of control sexual behavior: Rethinking sex addiction.* New York, NY: Springer.

Briere, J., & Gil, E. (1998). Self-mutilation in clinical and general population samples: Prevalence, correlates, and functions. *American Journal of Orthopsychiatry, 68*, 609–620. doi: 10.1037/h0080369.

Bronheim, H. E. (1998). *Body and soul: The role of object relations in faith, shame, and healing.* Northvale, NJ: Jason Aronson.

Brown, L. S. (1990). What's addiction got to do with it: A feminist critique of codependence. *Psychology of Women, 17*, 1–4.

Brown, T. O. (2010). *"If someone finds out you're a perv": The experience and management of stigma in the BDSM subculture.* (Unpublished doctoral dissertation). Ohio University.

Byers, E. S., & Rehman, U. S., (2014). *Sexual well-being.* In D. L. Tolman, L. M. Diamond, J. A. Bauermeister, W. H. George, J. G. Pfaus, L. M. Ward, (Eds.), *APA handbook of sexuality and psychology, Vol. 1: Person-based approaches. APA handbooks in psychology.* (pp. 317–337). Washington, DC: American Psychological Association.

Califia, P. (2001). *Sensuous magic: A guide to S/M for adventurous couples.* Berkeley, CA: Cleis Press.

Cameron, J. J., & Ross, M. (2007). In times of uncertainty: Predicting the survival of long-distance relationships. *Journal of Social Psychology, 147*(6), 581–606.

Chirinos, P. (2015). *Changing Taboos: Healthy sexuality today.* Paper presented at the Northern Virginia Licensed Professional Counselors Seminar.

Chirinos, P., & Shahbaz, C. (2015). *Unspeakable violence: BDSM and abuse in GLBTQQI populations.* 20th Annual LGBTQI Psychotherapy Conference.

Claes, L., Muehlenkamp, J., Vandereycken, W., Hamelinck, L., Martens, H., & Claes, S. (2010). Comparison of non-suicidal self-injurious behavior and suicide attempts in patients admitted to a psychiatric crisis unit. *Personality and Individual Differences, 48,* 83–87. doi: 10.1016/j.paid.2009.09.00.

Coleman, E. (1982). Developmental stages of the coming out process. *Journal of Homosexuality, 7*(2–3), 31–43.

Connolly, P. H. (2006). Psychological functioning of bondage/domination/sadomasochism (BDSM) practitioners. *Journal of Psychology & Human Sexuality, 18*(1), 79–120.

Cross, P. A., & Matheson K. (2006). Understanding sadomasochism an empirical examination of four perspectives. *Journal of Homosexuality, 50*(2/3), 133–166.

Crouch, W., & Wright, J. (2004). Deliberate self-harm at an adolescent unit: A qualitative investigation. *Clinical Child Psychology and Psychiatry, 9*(2), 185–204.

Csíkszentmihályi, M. (1991). *Flow: The psychology of optimal experience.* New York, NY: Harper Collins.

Cutler, B. (2003). *Partner selection, power dynamics, and sexual bargaining in self-defined BDSM couples.* (Unpublished doctoral dissertation.) The Institute for Advanced Study of Human Sexuality, San Francisco, CA.

Dancer, P. L., Kleinplatz, P. J., & Moser, C. (2006). 24/7 SM slavery. *Journal of Homosexuality, 2/3,* 81–101.

Davis, R. L. (2008). *Domestic violence: Intervention, prevention, policies, and solutions.* Boca Raton, FL: CRC Press.

Deri, J. H. (2011). *Polyamory or polyagony? Jealousy in open relationships.* (Unpublished doctoral dissertation).

Dietrich, A. (2003). Functional neuroanatomy of altered states of consciousness: The transient hypofrontality hypothesis. *Consciousness and Cognition, 12*(2), 231–256.

Downing, L. (2015). Heteronormativity and repronormativity in sexological "perversion theory" and the DSM-5's "paraphilic disorder" diagnoses. *Archives of Sexual Behavior, 44*(5), 1139–1145.

Drescher, J., & Merlino, J. P. (2007). *American psychiatry and homosexuality: An oral history.* New York, NY: Harrington Park Press.

Dutton, D.G., & Corvo, K. (2007). Corrigendum to "Transforming a flawed policy: A call to revive psychology and science in domestic violence research and practice." *Aggression and Violent Behavior, 12*(20), 257. doi:10.1016/j.avb.2006.01.007.

Easton, D., & Liszt, C. (2000). *When someone you love is kinky.* Eugene, OR: Greenery Press.

Emery, R. E. (2013). *Cultural sociology of divorce: An encyclopedia*. Thousand Oaks, CA: SAGE Reference.

Fay, D., Haddadi, H., Seto, M. C., Wang, H., & Kling, C. (2016). An exploration of fetish social networks and communities. In *Advances in Network Science* (pp. 195–204). New York, NY: Springer International Publishing.

Finley, L. L. (2013). *Encyclopedia of domestic violence and abuse*. Santa Barbara, CA: ABC-CLIO.

First, M. B. (2014). DSM-5 and paraphilic disorders. *Journal of the American Academy of Psychiatry and the Law Online. 42*(2), 191–201.

Foucault, M., (1978). *The history of sexuality*. New York, NY: Pantheon Books.

Franklin, J. C., Aaron, R. V., Arthur, M. S., Shorkey, S., & Prinstein, M. J. (2012). Nonsuicidal selfinjury and diminished pain perception: The role of emotion dysregulation. *Comprehensive Psychiatry, 53*, 691–700. doi: 10.1016/j.comppsych.2011.11.008.

Freud, S., & Strachey, J. (1975). *Three essays on the theory of sexuality*. New York, NY: Basic Books.

Fulkerson, A. (2010). *Bound by consent: Concepts of consent within the leather and bondage, domination, sadomasochism (BDSM) communities* (Unpublished doctoral dissertation). Wichita State University, Wichita, KS.

Gahr, M., Plener, P. L., Kölle, M. A., Freudenmann, R. W., & Schönfeldt-Lecuona, C. (2012). Self-mutilation induced by psychotropic substances: A systematic review. *Psychiatry Research, 200*(2), 977–983.

Gallagher, B., & Wilson, A. (1984). Michael Foucault, an interview: Sex, power, and the politics of identity. *Advocate Issue 400*, p. 26.

Gierymski, T., & Williams, T. (1986). Codependency. *Journal of Psychoactive Drugs, 18*(1), 7–13.

Gilbert, R. L., Gonzalez, M. A., & Murphy, N. A. (2011). Sexuality in the 3D Internet and its relationship to real-life sexuality. *Psychology & Sexuality, 2*(2), 107–122.

Glucklich, A. (2001). *Sacred pain: Hurting the body for the sake of the soul*. Oxford, UK: Oxford University Press.

Glyde, T. (2015). BDSM: Psychotherapy's grey area. *The Lancet Psychiatry, 2*(3), 211–213.

Gonzales, A. H., & Bergstrom, L. (2013). Adolescent non-suicidal self-injury (NSSI) interventions. *Journal of Child & Adolescent Psychiatric Nursing, 26*(2), 124–130. doi-10.1111/jcap.12035.

Graham, B. C., Butler, S. E., McGraw, R., Cannes, S. M., & Smith, J. (2015). Member perspectives on the role of BDSM communities. *Journal of Sex Research*, 1–15.

Grof, S. (2008). Brief history of transpersonal psychology. *International Journal of Transpersonal Studies, 27*, 46–54.

Grof, S., International Transpersonal Association, & International Transpersonal Conference. (1985). *East & west: Ancient wisdom and modern science*. San Francisco, CA: Robert Briggs Associates.

Guidroz, K. (2008). "Are you top or bottom?": Social science answers for everyday questions about sadomasochism. *Sociology Compass, 2*(6), 1766–1782.

Haber, M. (2013, March 7). A hush-hush topic no more. *The New York Times*. Retrieved from www.nytimes.com.

Haley, D. (2014). Bound by law: A roadmap for the practical legalization of BDSM. *Cardozo JL & Gender, 21*, 631.

Hammers, C. (2014). Corporeality, sadomasochism and sexual trauma. *Body & Society, 20*(2), 68–90.

Hancock, R., McAuliffe, G., & Levingston, K. (2014). Factors impacting counselor competency with sexual minority intimate partner violence victims. *Journal of LGBT Issues in Counseling, 8*(1), 74–94. DOI: 10.1080/15538605.2014.853640.

Hanmer, J., & Itzin, C. (2000). *Home truths about domestic violence: Feminist influences on policy and practice: A reader.* London, UK: Routledge.

Harrington, L. (2011). *Sacred kink: The eightfold paths of BDSM and beyond.* Mystic Productions: Lynwood, WA.

Hartelius, G., Caplan, M., & Rardin, M. A. (2007). Transpersonal psychology: Defining the past, divining the future. *The Humanistic Psychologist, 35*(2), 135– 160. doi:10.1080/08873260701274017.

Hébert, A., & Weaver, A. (2015). Perks, problems, and the people who play: A qualitative exploration of dominant and submissive BDSM roles. *Canadian Journal of Human Sexuality, 24*(1), 49–62.

Hellmuth, J. C., Follansbee, K. W., Moore, T. M., & Stuart, G. L. (2008). Reduction of intimate partner violence in a gay couple following alcohol treatment. *Journal of Homosexuality, 54*(4), 439–448.

Henderson, J. L. (1990). *Shadow and self: Selected papers in analytical psychology.* Wilmette, IL: Chiron Publications.

Herlihy, B., & Corey, G. (2014). *ACA ethical standards casebook.* New York, NY: John Wiley & Sons.

Herpertz, S. (1995). Self-injurious behavior: Psychopathological and nosological characteristics in subtypes of self-injurers. *Acta Psychiatrica Scandinavica, 91*(1), 57–68. doi: 10.1111/j.1600-0447.1995.tb09743.x.

Hertlein, K. M., & Piercy, F. P. (2006). Internet infidelity: A critical review of the literature. *The Family Journal, 14*(4), 366–371.

Hillman, J. (1975). *Re-visioning psychology.* New York, NY: Harper Perennial.

Hillman, J., & Ventura, M. (1992). *We've had a hundred years of psychotherapy – And the world's getting worse.* San Francisco, CA: HarperSanFrancisco.

Hoff, G., & Sprott, R. A. (2009). Therapy experiences of clients with BDSM sexualities: Listening to a stigmatized sexuality. *Electronic Journal of Human Sexuality, 12*(9), 30.

Holt, K. (2016). Blacklisted: Boundaries, violations, and retaliatory behavior in the BDSM community. *Deviant Behavior, 37*(8), 917–930.

Hooley, J. M., Ho, D. T., Slater, J., & Lockshin, A. (2010). Pain perception and non-suicidal selfinjury: A laboratory investigation. *Personality Disorders: Theory, Research, and Treatment, 7*, 170–179. doi: 10.1037/a0020106.

Hsu, B., Kling, A., Kessler, C., Knapke, K., Diefenbach, P., & Elias, J. E. (1994). Gender differences in sexual fantasy and behavior in a college population: A ten-year replication. *Journal of Sex & Marital Therapy, 20*, 103–118.

Humes, A. (1989, November 1). The culting of codependency. In C. M. Renzetti & C. H. Miley (Eds.) *Violence in gay and lesbian domestic partnerships* (pp. 61–68). New York, NY: Harrington Park Press.

Iannotti, L. (2014). I didn't consent to that: Secondary analysis of discrimination against BDSM identified individuals. *CUNY Academic Works.*

James, E. L., & Random House. (2011). *Fifty shades of Grey.* New York, NY: Random House Large Print.

Janus, S. S., & Janus, C. L. (1993). *The Janus report on sexual behavior.* Oxford, UK: John Wiley & Sons.

Joyal, C., & Carpenter, J. (2016). The prevalence of paraphilic interests and behaviors in the general population: A provincial survey. *Journal of Sex Research*, July, 3, 1–11.

Joyce, P., & Sills, C. (2001). *Skills in gestalt counselling and psychotherapy.* London, UK: SAGE.

Jozifkova, E. (2013). Consensual sadomasochistic sex (BDSM): The roots, the risks, and the distinctions between BDSM and violence. *Current Psychiatry Reports, 15*(9), 1–8.

Jung, C. G. (1953). H. Read, M. Fordham, & G. Adler (Eds.). *The collected works of C. G. Jung.* New York, NY: Pantheon Books.

Kaldera, R. (2006). *Dark moon rising: Pagan BDSM and the Ordeal Path.* Hubbardston, MA: Asphodel Press.

Kaldera, R. (2010). *Power circuits: Polyamory in a power dynamic.* Hubbardston, MA: Alfred Press.

Kaldera, R., & Popp, S. (2014). *Unequal by design: Counseling power dynamic relationships.* Hubbardston, MA: Alfred Press.

Kaldera, R., & Tashlin, D. (2013a). *Broken toys: Submissives with mental illness or neurological dysfunction.* Hubbardston, MA: Alfred Press.

Kaldera, R., & Tashlin, D. (2013b) *Mastering mind: Dominants with mental illness or neurological dysfunction.* Hubbardston, MA: Alfred Press.

Kelmer, G., Rhoades, G. K., Stanley, S., & Markman, H. J. (2013). Relationship quality, commitment, and stability in long-distance relationships. *Family Process, 52*(2), 257–270.

Kelsey, K., Stiles, B. L., Spiller, L., & Diekhoff, G. M. (2013). Assessment of therapists' attitudes towards BDSM. *Psychology & Sexuality, 4*(3), 255–267.

Khan, U. (2009). A woman's right to be spanked: Testing the limits of tolerance of SM in the socio-legal imaginary. *Law & Sexuality: A Review of Lesbian, Gay, Bisexual, & Transgender Legal Issues, 18*, 79.

Khan, U. (2014). *Vicarious kinks: S/m in the socio-legal imaginary.* Toronto: University of Toronto Press.

Khan, U. (2015). Sadomasochism in sickness and in health: Competing claims from science, social science, and culture. *Current Sexual Health Reports, 7*(1), 49–58.

Klein, K., Holtby, A., Cook, K., & Travers, R. (2015). Complicating the coming out narrative: Becoming oneself in a heterosexist and cissexist world. *Journal of Homosexuality, 62*(3), 297–326.

Klein, M., & Moser, C. (2006). SM (sadomasochistic) interests as an issue in a child custody proceeding. *Journal of Homosexuality, 2/3*, 233–242.

Kleinplatz, P., & Moser, C. (2004). Toward clinical guidelines for working with BDSM clients. *Contemporary Sexuality, 38*(6), 1, 4–5.

Kleinplatz, P. J., & Moser, C. (2005). Is S/M pathological? *Lesbian & Gay Psychology Review, 6*, 255–260.

Kleinplatz, P. J., & Moser, C. (2006). *Sadomasochism: Powerful pleasures.* New York, NY: Harrington Park Press.

Klesse, C. (2014). Polyamory: Intimate practice, identity or sexual orientation? *Sexualities, 17*(1–2), 81–99.

Klonsky, E. D. (2009). The functions of self-injury in young adults who cut themselves: Clarifying the evidence for affect-regulation. *Psychiatry Research, 766*(2– 3), 260–268. doi: 10.1016/j.psychres.2008.02.008.

Klonsky, E. D., & Muehlenkamp, J. J. (2007). Self-injury: A research review for the practitioner. *Journal of Clinical Psychology, 63*(11), 1045–1056.

Knight, E. (2014). In search of the centaur. *Journal of Integral Theory & Practice, 9*(1), 88–98.

Kolmes, K., Stock, C., & Moser, C. (2006). Investigating bias in psychotherapy with BDSM clients. *Journal of Homosexuality, 50*(2–3), 301–324.

Krafft-Ebing, R. (1886). *Psychopathia sexualis: Eine klinisch-forensische Studie.* Stuttgart: Enke.

Krestan, J., & Bepko, C. (1990). Codependency: The social reconstruction of female experience. *Smith College Studies in Social Work, 60,* 216–232.

Kristeva, J. (2001). *Melanie Klein.* New York, NY: Columbia University Press.

Labriola, K. (2010). *Love in abundance: A counselor's guide to open relationships.* Eugene, OR: Greenery Press.

Langdridge, D. (2006). Voices from the margins: Sadomasochism and sexual citizenship. *Citizenship Studies, 10*(4), 373–389.

Langdridge, D., & Barker, M. (2007). *Safe, sane and consensual: Contemporary perspectives on sadomasochism.* Houndmills: Palgrave MacMillan.

Lawrence A. A., & Love Crowell, J. (2008). Psychotherapists' experience with clients who engage in consensual sadomasochism: A qualitative study. *Journal of Sex & Marital Therapy, 34,* 67–85.

Lawson, J. (2012). Sociological theories of intimate partner violence. *Journal of Human Behavior in the Social Environment, 22*(5), 572–590.

Lee, E. M., Klement, K., R., Ambler, J. K., Loewald, T., Comber, E., Hanson, S. A., Pruitt, B., & Sagarin, B. J. (2016). Altered states of consciousness during an extreme ritual. *PLOS ONE, 11*(5), e0153126.

Leistner, C. E., & Mark, K. P. (2016). Fifty shades of sexual health and BDSM identity messaging: A thematic analysis of the *Fifty Shades* series. *Sexuality & Culture, 20*(8), 464–485.

Levine, R., & Shahbaz, C. (2010). *Becoming a "kink aware" therapist or, what to do when the leather vest and chaps walk in.* Paper presented at Los Angeles Gay & Lesbian psychotherapy Association, Los Angeles, CA.

Lewis, A. (2012). Just your average Joe: Getting to know a lifestyle kinkster. *Counselling Australia, 11*(2), 1–8.

Lex, B. W. (1976). Physiological aspects of ritual trance. *Journal of Altered States of Consciousness, 2*(2), 109–122.

Lin, K. (2014). *The demedicalization of kink: Social change and shifting contexts of sexual politics.* (Unpublished doctoral dissertation). University of Delaware.

Linehan, M. M. (2000). Behavioral treatments of suicidal behaviors: Definitional obfuscation and treatment outcomes. In R. W. Maris, S. S. Cannetto, J. L. McIntosh, & M. M. Siverman (Eds.), *Review of Suicidology* (pp. 84–111). New York, NY: Guilford Press.

Lukoff, D. (2012). Review of Bodymind healing psychotherapy. Ancient pathways to modern health and energy psychology: Self-healing practices for bodymind health. *Journal of Transpersonal Psychology, 44*(1), 109–112.

Maddux, J. E., & Winstead, B. A. (2012). *Psychopathology: Foundations for a contemporary understanding.* New York, NY: Routledge.

Magliano, J. (2015). The surprising psychology of BDSM. The wide wide world of psychology: *Psychology Today,* 2015-2.

Mains, G. (1984). *Urban aboriginals: A celebration of leather sexuality.* Miami, FL: Gay Sunshine Press.

Marrs, S. A., & Staton, A. R. (2016). Negotiating difficult decisions: Coming out vs. passing in the workplace. *Journal of LGBT Issues in Counseling, 10*(1), 40–54. DOI: 10.1080/15538605.2015.1138097.

Martin, R. J., Borneman, J., Boon, J., Clark-Deces, I., Greenhouse, C., & Princeton University. (2011). Powerful exchanges: Ritual and subjectivity in Berlin's BDSM scene. *Dissertation Abstracts International, 73–2*. Retrieved from http://arks.princeton.edu/ark:/88435/dsp01qz20ss51g.

Masters, P. (2009). *The control book*. Customs Books Publishing.

McCabe, C. S. (2015). *Facebook for kinky people: A discursive analysis of Fetlife*. (Unpublished doctoral dissertation).

McKee, A. (2005). The need to bring the voices of pornography consumers into public debates about the genre and its effects. *Australian Journal of Communication, 32*(2), 71.

Meeker, C. (2011). Bondage and discipline, dominance and submission, and sadism and masochism (BDSM) identity development. In M. S. Plakhotnik, S. M. Nielsen, & D. M. Pane (Eds.), *Proceedings of the Tenth Annual College of Education & GSN Research Conference* (pp. 154–161). Miami: Florida International University. Retrieved from http://coeweb.fiu.edu/research_conference/.

Midori (2005). *Wild side sex: The book of kink*. Los Angeles, CA: Daedalus.

Mileham, B. L. A. (2007). Online infidelity in Internet chat rooms: An ethnographic exploration. *Computers in Human Behavior, 23*(1), 11–31.

Miller, P., & Devon, M. (1995). *Screw the roses, send me the thorns: The romance and sexual sorcery of sadomasochism*. Fairfield, CT: Mystic Rose Books.

Moore, T. (1990). *Dark eros: The imagination of sadism*. Spring Publications.

Moser, C. (2006). Demystifying alternative sexual behaviors. *Sexuality, Reproduction and Menopause, 4*(2), 86–90.

Moser, C., & Kleinplatz, P. J. (2006). Introduction: The state of our knowledge on SM. *Journal of Homosexuality, 2/3*, 1–15.

Moss, D. (1999). *Humanistic and transpersonal psychology: A historical and biographical sourcebook*. Westport, CT: Greenwood Press.

Moulds, J. (2015). Is society still shackled with the chains of a 1993 England? Consent, sado-masochism and R v Brown. *UniSA Student Law Review, 1*.

Muehlenkamp, J. J. (2006). Empirically supported treatments and general therapy guidelines for non-suicidal self-injury. *Journal of Mental Health Counseling, 28*(2), 166–185.

Muehlenkamp, J., Claes, L., Havertape, L., & Plener, P. (2012). International prevalence of adolescent non-suicidal self-injury and deliberate selfharm. *Child and Adolescent Psychiatry and Mental Health, 6*, 1–9. doi: 10.1186/1753-2000-6-10.

Murray, C. E., & Mobley, A. K. (2009). Empirical research about same-sex intimate partner violence: A methodological review. *Journal of Homosexuality, 56*(3), 361–386.

Musser, A. J. (2015). BDSM and the boundaries of criticism: Feminism and neoliberalism in *Fifty Shades of Grey* and *The Story of O*. *Feminist Theory, 16*(2), 121–136.

National Coalition for Sexual Freedom (NCSF). (1998). SM vs. Abuse. Retrieved from www.ncsfreedom.org/library/smvsabuse.htm.

Newmahr, S. (2010). Rethinking kink: Sadomasochism as serious leisure. *Qualitative Sociology, 33*, 313–331.

Nichols, M. (2005). Psychotherapeutic issues with 'Kinky' clients clinical problems, yours and theirs. *Journal of Homosexuality, 50*, 281–300.

Nichols, M. (2013). Psychology & BDSM: Pathology or individual difference. Institute for personal growth. Retrieved from www.ipgcounseling.com/sites/ipgcounseling.com/files/content/pdf/3psychology_bdsm.pdf.

Nichols, M. (2014). Couples and kinky sexuality: The need for a new therapeutic approach. In *Critical Topics in Family Therapy* (pp. 139–149). Heidelberg, Germany: Springer International Publishing.

Nietzsche, F. W., Kaufmann, W. A., & Hollingdale, R. J. (1967). *The will to power.* New York, NY: Random House.

O'Gorman, P. (1990). Developmental aspects of codependency. *Counselor Magazine,* March–April, 14–16.

O'Gorman, P. (1993). Codependency explored – A social movement in search of definition and treatment. *Psychiatric Quarterly, 64*(2), 199–212. doi-10.1007/ BF01065870.

O'Gorman, P., Oliver-Diaz, P. (1987). *Breaking the cycle of addiction for adult children of alcoholics.* Deerfield Beach, FL: Health Communications.

Ortmann, D. M., & Sprott, R. A. (2013). *Sexual outsiders: Understanding BDSM sexualities and communities.* Lanham, MD: Rowman & Littlefield.

Pa, M. (2001). Beyond the pleasure principle: The criminalization of consensual sadomasochistic sex. *Texas Journal of Women & Law, 11*(1), 51–89.

Palandri, M., & Green, L. (2000). Image management in a bondage, discipline, sadomasochist subculture: A cyber-ethnographic study. *CyberPsychology & Behavior, 3*(4), 631–641.

Parrott, W. G., & Smith, R. H. (1993). Distinguishing the experiences of envy and jealousy. *Journal of Personality and Social Psychology, 64,* 906–920.

Partridge, E., Dalzell, T., & Victor, T. (2006). *The new Partridge dictionary of slang and unconventional English.* London, UK: Routledge.

Pillai-Friedman, S., Pollitt, J. L., & Castaldo, A. (2015). Becoming kink-aware – A necessity for sexuality professionals. *Sexual and Relationship Therapy, 30*(2), 196–210.

Pitagora, D. (2016). The kink-poly confluence: Relationship intersectionality in marginalized communities. *Sexual and Relationship Therapy, 31*(3), 391–405.

Powers, H. J. (2007). *Bias in psychotherapy with BDSM clients and BDSM in psychotherapy: A culturally aware curriculum.* (Unpublished paper). California State University.

Powls, J., & Davies, J. (2012). A descriptive review of research relating to sadomasochism: Considerations for clinical practice. *Deviant Behavior, 33*(3), 223–234.

Prior, E. E. (2015). Domination and submission (D&S). In P. Whelehan & A. Bolin (Eds.), *The International Encyclopedia of Human Sexuality.* West Sussex, UK: Wiley-Blackwell. DOI: 10.1002/9781118896877.wbiehs117.

Proust, M. (1929). *The captive.* C.K. Scott Moncrieff (Trans). London, UK: A.A. Knopf.

Rabby, M. K. (2007). Relational maintenance and the influence of commitment in online and offline relationships. *Communication Studies, 58*(3), 315–337.

Rambukkana, N. (2007). Taking the leather out of leathersex: The Internet, identity, and the sadomasochistic public sphere. In K. O'Riordan & D. J. Phillips (Eds.), *Queer online: Media technology & sexuality* (p. 67–80). New York, NY: Peter Lang.

Ramsour, P. J. (2002). *Masochism, sexual freedom, and radical democracy: A hermeneutic study of sadomasochism in psychoanalytic, sociological, and contemporary texts.* (Unpublished dissertation). Vanderbilt University, Nashville, TN.

Reinisch, J. M., Beasley, R., Kent, D., & Kinsey Institute for Research in Sex, Gender, and Reproduction. (1990). *The Kinsey Institute new report on sex: What you must know to be sexually literate.* New York, NY: St. Martin's Press.

Renzetti, C. M. (1996). The poverty of services for battered lesbians. In C. M. Renzetti & C. H. Miley (Eds.), *Violence in gay and lesbian domestic partnerships* (pp. 61–68). New York, NY: Harrington Park Press.

Richters, J., De Visser, R. O., Rissel, C. E., Grulich, A. E., & Smith, A. (2008). Demographic and psychosocial features of participants in bondage and discipline, "sadomasochism" or dominance and submission (BDSM): Data from a national survey. *Journal of Sexual Medicine, 5*(7), 1660–1668.

Richters, J., Grulich, A. E., de Visser, R. O., Smith, A. M., & Rissel, C. E. (2003). Sex in Australia: Autoerotic, esoteric and other sexual practices engaged in by a representative sample of adults. *Australian and New Zealand Journal of Public Health, 27*, 180–190.

Ridley, C. A., & Feldman, C. M. (2003). Female domestic violence toward male partners – exploring conflict responses and outcomes. *Journal of Family Violence, 18*(3), 157–170. doi-10.1023/A-1023516521612.

Rinella, J., & Bean, J. W. (1994). *The master's manual: A handbook of erotic dominance.* Los Angeles, CA: Daedalus

Rivoli, L. R. (2015). Liberation through Domination: BDSM culture and submissive-role women. *Student Publications. Paper 318.* Retrieved from http://cupola. gettysburg.edu/student_scholarship/318.

Rodemaker, D. (2008). *Altsex: The clinician's guide to BDSM.* (Unpublished doctoral dissertation). Chicago School of Professional Psychology, Chicago, IL.

Rogers, C. (1979). *On becoming a person: A therapist's view of psychotherapy.* London, UK: Constable.

Ross, A. D. (2012). Revisiting the body in pain: The rhetoric of modern masochism. *Sexuality & Culture, 16*(3), 230–240.

Rubel, R. J. (2008). *Protocol handbook for the leather slave: Theory and practice.* Las Vegas, NV: Nazca Plains Corp.

Rubel, R. J., & Fairfield, M. J. (2014). *BDSM mastery-relationships: A guide for creating mindful relationships for dominants and submissives.* Austin, TX: Red Eight Ball Press.

Rubel, R. J., & Fairfield, M. J. (2015). *Master/slave Mastery – Advanced: Rekindling the fire, ideas that matter.* Austin, TX: Red Eight Ball Press.

Rubel, R. J., & Wiseman, J. (2006). *Master/slave relations: Handbook of theory and practice.* Las Vegas, NV: Nazca Plains Corp.

Russ, M. J., Roth, S. D., Lerman, A., Kakuma, T., Harrison, K., Shindledecker, R. D., & Mattis, S. (1992). Pain perception in self-injurious patients with borderline personality disorder. *Biological Psychiatry, 32*, 501–511. Retrieved from http://dx.doi.org/10.1016/0006-3223(92)90218-0.

Sagarin, B. J., Cutler, B., Cutler, N., Lawler-Sagarin, K. A., & Matuszewich, L. (2009). Hormonal changes and couple bonding in consensual sadomasochistic activity. *Archives of Sexual Behavior, 38*, 186–200.

Sagarin, B. J., Lee, E. M., & Klement, K. R. (2015). Sadomasochism without sex? Exploring the parallels between BDSM and extreme rituals. *Journal of Positive Sexuality, 1*, 32–36.

Said, E. W. (1979). *Orientalism.* New York, NY: Vintage Books.

Sandnabba, K. N., Santtila, L. A., & Nordling, N. (2002). Demographics, sexual behavior, family background and abuse experiences of practitioners of sadomasochistic sex: A review of recent research. *Sexual and Relationship Therapy, 17*, 39–55.

Schussler, A. (2013). Pornography and postmodernism. *Postmodern Openings*, *4*(3), 7–23.

Seneca, L. A., & Hadas, M. (1968). *The stoic philosophy of Seneca: Essays and letters of Seneca*. New York, NY: W.W. Norton.

Shahbaz, C. (2008). *The beast within: A critique of Freud's view of sadomasochism*. (Unpublished paper). Pacifica Graduate Institute.

Shahbaz, C. (2009a). *The kinky psyche: Seeing sadomasochistic master slave dynamics through a Hillmanian perspective*. (Unpublished paper). Pacifica Graduate Institute.

Shahbaz, C. (2009b). *Seeing into extreme sadomasochism: Interviews with practitioners*. (Unpublished fieldwork paper). Pacifica Graduate Institute.

Shahbaz, C. (2010). *Shamanism and SM: Ethnographic voices from the field*. (Unpublished paper). Pacifica Graduate Institute.

Shahbaz C., (2012a). *Kinkophobia. Harmful Psychiatric Diagnosis: A call to action*. Paper given at Psychologists for Social Responsibility conference, Washington, DC.

Shahbaz C. (2012b). *Masters from Mars, Masters from Venus: Gender differences in Master slave dynamics*. (Unpublished paper). Pacifica Graduate Institute.

Shahbaz, C., & Rodemaker, D. (2012). *Beyond consent: A new paradigm for abuse in Master slave relationships*. 5th Annual Alternative Sexualities Conference, Chicago, Illinois.

Shannon, J. B. (2009). *Domestic violence sourcebook: Basic consumer health information about warning signs, risk factors, and health consequences of intimate partner violence, sexual violence and rape, stalking, human trafficking, child maltreatment, teen dating violence, and elder abuse: along with facts about victims and perpetrators, strategies for violence prevention, and emergency interventions, safety plans, and financial and legal tips for victims, a glossary of related terms, and directories of resources for additional information and support*. Detroit, MI: Omnigraphics.

Sheff, E., & Hammers, C. (2011). The privilege of perversities: Race, class and education among polyamorists and kinksters. *Psychology & Sexuality*, *2*(3), 198–223.

Silva, A. D. (2015). *Through pain, more gain? A survey into the psychosocial benefits of sadomasochism*. (Master's thesis). University of Oslo. Retrieved from http://urn.nb.no/URN:NBN:no-52512.

Silverstein, C. (2009). The implications of removing homosexuality from the DSM as a mental disorder. *Archives of Sexual Behavior*, *38*(2), 161–163. doi:10.1007/s10508-008-9442-x.

Sisson, K. (2007). The cultural formation of S/M: History and analysis. In D. Langdridge & M. Barker (Eds.), *Safe, sane and consensual: Contemporary perspectives on sadomasochism* (pp. 10–34). New York, NY: Palgrave.

Stein, D., Schachter, D., & Bean, J. W. (2009). *Ask the man who owns him: The real lives of gay masters and slaves*. New York, NY: Perfectbound Press.

Stroehmer, R., Edel, M. A., Pott, S., Juckel, G., & Haussleiter, I. S. (2015). Digital comparison of healthy young adults and borderline patients engaged in non-suicidal self-injury. *Annals of General Psychiatry*, *14*. http://doi.org/10.1186/s12991-015-0088-5.

Surprise, O. (2012). *Screaming green: A topography and Bourdieusian analysis of the model of sexual consent utilized by BDSM community members*. (Unpublished doctoral dissertation). Indiana University of Pennsylvania.

Taormino, T. (Ed.). (2012). *The ultimate guide to kink: BDSM, role play and the erotic edge.* Berkeley, CA: Cleis Press.

Taylor, B., & Davis, S. (2006). Using the extended PLISSIT model to address sexual healthcare needs. *Nursing Standard, 21*(11), 35–40.

Taylor, G. W., & Ussher, J. M. (2001). Making sense of S&M: A discourse analytic account. *Sexualities, 4,* 293–314.

Townsend, L. (1993). *The original leatherman's handbook.* Beverly Hills, CA: LT Publications.

Turley, E. L., King, N., & Butt, T. (2011). "It started when I barked once when I was licking his boots!": A descriptive phenomenological study of the everyday experience of BDSM. *Psychology & Sexuality, 2*(2), 123–136.

Vale, V., & Juno, A. (1989). *Modern primitives: An investigation of contemporary adornment & ritual.* San Francisco, CA: Re/Search Publications.

Van Der Walt, H. (2014). *Practitioner psychologists' understandings of bondage/discipline, dominance/submission, sadomasochism (BDSM): Shared or separate from those who practise it.* (Unpublished doctoral dissertation). Canterbury Christ Church University.

Voon, V., Mole, T. B., Banca, P., Porter, L., Morris, L., Mitchell, S., ... & Irvine, M. (2014). Neural correlates of sexual cue reactivity in individuals with and without compulsive sexual behaviours. *PLOS ONE, 9*(7), e102419.

Walters, J. W. (1990). The codependent Cinderella who loves too much ... fights back. *Family Therapy Networker, 14*(4), 53–57.

Warren, J. (1998). *The loving dominant.* New York, NY: Masquerade Books.

Weinberg, T. S. (1987). Sadomasochism in the United States: A review of recent sociological literature. *Journal of Sex Research, 23,* 50–69.

Weinberg, T. S. (2006). Sadomasochism and the social sciences: A review of the sociological and social psychological literature. *Journal of Homosexuality, 50*(2/3), 17–40.

Weiss, M. (2006) Mainstreaming kink: The politics of BDSM representation in U.S. popular media. *Journal of Homosexuality, 50*(2/3), 103–132.

Wetzel, J. W. (1991). Universal mental health classification systems: Reclaiming women's experience. *Affilia, 6*(3), 8–31.

Whitlock, J., Eckenrode, J., & Silverman, D. (2006). Self-injurious behaviors in a college population. *Pediatrics, 117,* 1939–1948. doi: 10.1542/peds.2005-2543.

Williams, D. J. (2006). Different (painful!) strokes for different folks: A general overview of sexual sadomasochism (SM) and its diversity. *Sexual Addiction & Compulsivity, 13*(4), 333–346.

Williams, D., Thomas, J., Prior, E., & Christensen, M. (2014). From "SSC" and "RACK" to the "4Cs": Introducing a new framework for negotiating BDSM participation. *Electronic Journal of Human Sexuality, 17.*

Winge, T. M. (2003). Constructing "neo-tribal" identities through dress: Modern primitives and body modifications (pp. 119–132). In K. Gelder, *The subcultures reader.* London, UK; New York, NY: Routledge.

Wiseman, J. (1996). *SM101: A realistic introduction.* 2nd edition. San Francisco, CA: Greenery Press.

Wismeijer, A., Van Assen, M. (2013). Psychological characteristics of BDSM practitioners. *Journal of Sexual Medicine, 10*(8), 1943–1952.

Wolfe, L. P. (2003). *Jealousy and transformation in polyamorous relationships* (Unpublished doctoral dissertation). The Institute for Advanced Study.

World Health Organization. (2006). *The world health report 2006: Working together for health*. Geneva: World Health Organization.

Wright, S. (2006). Discrimination of SM-identified individuals. *Journal of Homosexuality, 50*(2–3), 217–231.

Wright, S. (2010). Pathologizing consensual sexual sadism, sexual masochism, transvestic fetishism, and fetishism. *Archives of Sexual Behavior, 39*, 1229–1230.

Wright, S. (2014). Kinky parents and child custody: The effect of the DSM-5 differentiation between the paraphilias and paraphilic disorders. *Archives of Sexual Behavior, 43*(7), 1257–1258.

Wright, S. (2015). NCSF Incident Reporting & Response Annual Report. Retrieved from https://ncsfreedom.org/key-programs/incident-response/incident-response-reports.html.

You, J., Ma, C., Lin, M.P, & Leung, F. (2015). Comparing among the experiences of self-cutting, hitting, and scratching in Chinese adolescents attending secondary schools: An interview study. *Behavioral Disorders, 40*(2), 122–137.

Zila, L. M., & Kiselica, M. S. (2001). Understanding and counseling self-mutilation in female adolescents and young adults. *Journal of Counseling and Development, 79*, 46–53.

Zlotnick, C., Mattia, J. I., & Zimmerman, M. (1999). Clinical correlates of self-mutilation in a sample of general psychiatric patients. *Journal of Nervous and Mental Disease, 187*, 296–301. Retrieved from http://dx.doi.org/10.1097/00005053-199905000-00005.

About the Authors

Caroline Shahbaz has an extensive background in clinical psychology and holds a B.B.Sc. (Hons.), M.Psych., and an M.A. in Depth Psychology. Her research interests include exploring cultural, social, and professional persecution of marginalized alternative sexualities from a liberation and depth psychological perspective; understanding transformative aspects of BDSM practices and relationships; and bridging psychotherapeutic misunderstanding of alternative sexualities through ethnographic-based narratives. She has given presentations on issues related to the therapeutic aspects of BDSM practices/relationships, consensual Master/slave dynamics, kinkophobia, and difficulties in defining consent to a variety of professional and academic audiences.

© 2016 Diana Adams

Peter Chirinos's professional experience in the field of behavioral health began in 1993. He is a graduate of Gallaudet University, class of 1999. He has worked administratively and clinically in varied capacities, ranging from private clinical practice, community-based services agencies, inpatient and outpatient drug and alcohol treatment facilities, and emergency medical services response teams in a Level One trauma emergency department. Mr. Chirinos is the president and Chief Executive Officer of Capital Counseling Services, LLC, where he provides professional coaching and general psychotherapy services, as well as clinical treatment, training, and expert consultations in the area of sex, intimacy, and alternative sexualities. Online coaching and counseling services are provided utilizing state of the art web-based technology, while in-person, office-based services are provided in Arlington, Virginia. He identifies as a bisexual cisgender male living in a mixed-orientation marriage that is consensually non-monogamous.

Index

Printed in the United States
by Baker & Taylor Publisher Services